WALLS
OF THE
MIND

VOLUME 3:
(*Behind Open Doors.*)

By: Jonathan *W.* Haubert

Edited By: Jonathan W. Haubert

8	X	8

Order this book online at www.trafford.com
or email orders@trafford.com

Most Trafford titles are also available at major online book retailers.

Printed in the United States of America.

ISBN: 978-1-4669-7880-5 (sc)
ISBN: 978-1-4669-7881-2 (e)

Library of Congress Control Number: 2013901730

Because of the dynamic nature of the Internet, any web addresses or links contained in this book may have changed
since publication and may no longer be valid. The views expressed in this work are solely those of the author and do
not necessarily reflect the views of the publisher, and the publisher hereby disclaims any responsibility for them.

Any people depicted in stock imagery provided by Thinkstock are models,
and such images are being used for illustrative purposes only.
Certain stock imagery © Thinkstock.

Trafford rev. 12/26/2013

 www.trafford.com

North America & international
toll-free: 1 888 232 4444 (USA & Canada)
fax: 812 355 4082

The truth is - *there is no truth.*
Only the lie you choose to believe.

(Jonathan W. Haubert)

Wars of the Mind Contents:

Chapter 4 – *The Shortest Straw*

Chapter 7 – *The Turning Leaf*

Chapter 8 – *Casualty*

Chapter 11 – *One Day*

Chapter 1

Welcome In.

Regrets

Against smooth flesh, softly brushing its surface.
Yielding at the first signs of *"Grace and Glory."*
Slammed through and down to the spirit, now holding pride.
Left to wallow and shout to the night sky.

So face it clearly, give us *"Honor and Grace."*
Lord, of all that holds the bond of man and nature.
Give forth our meanings and poetic mounds of faith.
Kiss the nothing that stands between us.
Held calm and gently as we fade.

Exploding furiously in the eyes of the child's charm.
Held not to mean anything more for us to bear.
As it slides across and makes its way through.
Have we anything to state, other than truth?
Given and received, now growing between our faiths.
We must face the fact, that these are our fates to keep.

Up-Side

Go further than the streams, breaking all your hopes.
Go deeper into the ashes, and below all the notes.
Give forth our reasons, and love us till daybreak.
Left aside at the front, and waiting for you in shame...

Brought to attention, then it rains down over the child.
Left in the front, waiting for maybe some guidance.
Please give him an outlet, let him breathe again today.
The child wants only to live in the light.
To stand humble with God, *"For his soul to be saved."*

We've asked nothing more than to drink of the pure.
We've demanded nothing, other than to exist forevermore.
Go now further than the edge of our human natures and dreams.
Go one more step than your shadowed eyes can see...

Let the wind hold you up, as God whispers the way through.
Let these kisses keep you warm, held both calm and true.
Please allow this child to breathe again today.
Once God answers these questions.
"Our souls can then be saved."

Three Points

Ten thousand years away from ever knowing how.
A million times a day, it pushes and shouts.
Ever through and-round, in the deepest part of our souls.
Binding the lord's honor, taking the soldier home.

Ancient paint, now falling off from the frame.
Trivial words still ringing, through the child's brain.
Mother wants to save us, but we can never allow.
Give us our identities, then set them upon our crowns.

Father now holds the reason, *Lord* of all that continues the flow.
Still the other waits silent, "in darkness and all alone."
We venture now further, to prove what we already know.
Ever through and-round, in the deepest part of our souls.

Bind and break the temptations, then let mercy ring stiff.
So now it begins to sting us, burning just under the wrist.
So take it slowly and rhyme another sort of logic-break.
Between God and the Devil, humanity and this fate...

Set Not - Now Gone

Uneven, as it spills over this tongue.
No-reason left in the sink, burning till gone.
Mindless points to be made, when no one's home.
So to bite and gnaw at the phone line, "now all alone."

Justice flowing, in the open line to the *Far-Away.*
Embracing the moonlight, as the numbing songs pull you away.
Dreamless nights of when honor meant everything.
Now set off to the side, gone and no one can see...

Drifting down where no human can reach.
Left in the basement, "*Set not - Now gone.*"
Left in a wonder, drifting away with those songs.
So uneven, as it all spills over this tongue.
And so many mindless points to be made.
"When no one's home..."

Ratchet-Jaw

Twist it to the last point, then let it break.
Turn the handle to the left, but it won't just wait.
Take another *Mercy-Shot*, then drown the shame in your eyes.
Please hold onto that one remaining thread.
Before we all fade back to the *Dark-Side*...

Hold up one hand if you're ready for rejoice.
Hold up your heart if you're ready to rest.
Lift your eyes to the heavens and stars.
Hold your breath, "because dreams can go far..."

Now push down onto the chain.
Bite-hard, and rip the shadow to the gray.
Lift only to see the face of their distorted Gods.
Now pull it another way, against the grain.
"And take these new points too far..."

Hold one hand up if you're ready for redemption.
Hold your hands together if you're ready to be judged.
Push not your anger onto the children.
Lift them to the heavens with your hearts.

Twist the wrong word, till it means something more.
Turn the handle to the left, bind-snap and now on the floor.
So be ready to shut the curtains and lock your door.
Forever now and just a little more.
Upon and through, all that meant something back then.
Now in the jaws of anger and remorse.
We took it too far once, now locked behind an open door.

Not Today

Above yet never to know.
Alone in the hollow, drifting with the embers and smoke.
Not meant to mean anything to you.
Still you lay awake, so confused.
I'm not ready to take you there with me.
I believe you're not ready to open your eyes to that dream.
Not ready until the song is done.
Not today – not till I'm gone.

Keep Me Going

Daylight fading, again now the sunlight falls away.
Endless, as all wonder leaves us behind.
"How many more miles must I go?"
Before this all subsides...

Taken now and reborn when the moon gives reason.
Left far beyond and at the beginning of a new sort of strive.
Was there ever a motive to this thing inside my head?
The voices ringing, still bringing me close to the edge.

Those vows still keep me going.
All of what I held means more now today.
It all keeps me afoot, and gets me out of the rain.
So far on and through so many pains.

It keeps me going...
Knowing that I'm still, "just at the start."
Please keep me going, take me to the stars...
Love me again the way you once did.
Please keep me going, far – far passed the end.

Remember?

Below all of the endless piles of paper and ink.
Through all the years of blood, sweat, tears and pain.
There is not much that rings more than this.
There is not much that keeps me alive.
Other than the fading thought of you and I...

But it takes more than just sweet words.
It means more than you would come to know.
But try as you may, to set it all straight.
And prove that "I" was indeed the monster in the end.

True, yet not ever to ring more than Pride.
Can you remember our first kiss and fight?
True to the end, but then it all fades.
Can you even remember, this hollow man's face?
The a*wesomeness,* of the life that I gave for you.
Will you ever remember, how much I had bled for you..?

Chance

Shoved under the sand, a million miles of grief.
Left under the shadow, in a daze of anger and disbelief.
Drowning in a pool, of what they call a Hollow-Shot.
Still here under the granite, giving chance a second thought.

Hopeless waiting for maybe a little kiss of faith.
Still waiting for time to take its toll and wipe away this fate.
Under and knowing, of how little a soul I have left.
Still I sit here alone, giving thought of that one last chance.

Broken under the rainfall, then washed away with the dirt.
Shoved under the notebook, erased and burned.
Left alone in a ponder, of how I seem to destroy all.
How long must I wander, through the cold and frost?

Still anger is steaming, seeming to know no bounds.
So many miles, under the sea but never will I drown...?
Left in a pool, of what they call an empty shot.
Still under the granite, giving chance a second thought.

Waiting...

Go ahead and call it...
If you wish to live a lie and dwell in shame.
Go ahead and lock it...
Because you know it will never be the same.

Memories of all that rings numb.
Still fighting for a chance to make this right.
Pointless hatred, shoved deep into your lungs at night.

Then salt stands as a brick.
Keeping the two points from ever becoming one.
There's nothing the angel can do now.
"Just weep and load the gun."

Soon an ending, when God gives the command.
That's why I've been waiting here.
Forever under the dirt, dust and ash...

Restless

No one answers, as I call out into the night.
No one's there, to guide me out and to the light.
Night-fall has given, and still I have nothing but this.
How many times must I fall, before I can hit..?

Awake in the morning - still day holds the gift.
Of so many tears I have given.
"Endlessly they fall into the abyss."

Night-break has taken, all my hopes into the grave.
But you shouldn't worry, for a soul that shall never be saved.
And still it's haunting, I just can't seem to escape.
So I think I can just let go for now.
Still restless, I lie awake...

Voice Of Ember

Light falls through, the raindrop now frozen.
Passion pulls through, and fate pauses for a moment.
Tell us that love wasn't true, and take this heartbeat away.
Hold the key to the sky and see what stands on the other side...

Rapid teardrops beating onto the concrete.
Smoke now subsides, showing only a tired dream.
Correction of the defect, held as "*Human Nature.*"
It dances in our hopes, and strolls through the graveyard.

Sweet little nothings that our minds need not know.
Dancing upon the shadow, lifting above the smoke.
It pushes aside the nightmare, and holds us down to this.
It dances behind our eyes, leading to the abyss.

Unwilling but still a little nauseous.
Unyielding and never to give more than that.
The voice, it sings its song to our souls.
Guiding the way back to the grave.
It takes its time and holds us calm.
Leading us to the other side, of this fleeting day...

Child Fears

So long in the waiting, still hoping someone will care.
The child still dreams of forgetting.
Only to lie awake in his eternal despair.

Fate called the moment.
Then it all slipped to the side – away.
Still he waits for morning.
"Forever the dreamer lies awake..."

Stuck in the middle.
There was once a line drawn, now only ash.
He lies awake in the knowing.
That his nightmares will never pass.

So long in the hoping, still giving *Grace* a chance.
The child dreams of forgetting.
"Yet knows his fears will never pass..."

Head-Ache

Nothing seems to stop it.
Soon it will take control and end the light.
Nothing seems to heal it.
Please give me strength to end this night.

Walls spinning, taking me deep into the ground.
Now my body freezing.
"This pain knows no bounds."

Frantic-frenzied-fortitude-failing.
Blind-bold-belligerent-bailing.
Sore-sanctioned-steaming-sorrow.
Mindless pointless dreams of tomorrow...

Non-stop thoughts of redemption.
Endless mounds of my meaningless strive.
My head will never stop pounding.
So pull the trigger, and turn out the lights...

"Turn out the lights..."

Shot in the Dark

Maybe on another level.
Somehow you'll find out what it means.
Maybe you could just wait for an answer.
Or just close your eyes and welcome the dream...

So take the hand of the monster.
Let him guide you to the lake.
Hold onto the wing of the angel.
Let the rain clean off the slate...

Hear the song of the dreamer.
Let the honor take you away.
Please hold your questions until this is over.
Now gone, done and buried away...

Clawing

So many scars.
I've lost count over the years.
So many broken hearts.
Drowning in these tears.

Miles away and so much un-said.
Hours a day, in and through my head.
It's been some time now.
But still the scar remains.
I could scrub all I want.
Yet forever I am stained.

So many tears.
Flowing over the edge.
So many years.
Echoes beating inside my head.

Never to subside, or fade with time.
It will never stop ringing.
Still these scars remain on the line.
And nothing will ever change it.
"I need now only to close my eyes..."

Elapsed

It's been some time now.
So many dreams gone and faded grim.
It's been so long now.
Yet still this hope stands upon a single whim.

Fright forgot, yet never lost.
Pain still beating, reminding us who we are.
Love now decayed, yet passion still rains.
Flooding the pool, held as our hearts...

The thoughts have passed.
Romance now elapsed.
Gone and faded when you wouldn't hold on.
It's been some time now.
And still you're gone...

This Taste

Not remembered, yet still it's here.
Forever left to splinter, breaking the tears.
Miles of heartache and so much left unsaid.
It's been so long now, and still we're dead...

Endless as it falls down.
Sinking below, to the bottom of the sea.
It's still so very far away.
Yet no one shall ever take this from me.

It's rising higher.
Damn this bitter taste in my throat.
It's lifting faster.
Soon I'll begin to choke.

Nothing nor no one.
Shall ever take away who I am.
And damn this taste, of the graveyard sands...

Knock – Knock!

Is someone there, standing at the end of the hall?
Does someone care, for this forgotten child's wants?
Will fate answer these questions?
Or am I left to seek what can never be found....?

Is anyone home, or am I by myself again?
Does anyone care, for this man's ignorant whims?
Please shuffle the last point, then let it go.
End this logic, far out and so unknown...

For no more reasons, only pride.
For only now, shall I rest my eyes.
So tell me - who's there, standing at the end of the hall.
Is anyone out there, or am I still lost...?

Bleeding Spirit

So now it's passing, forever grim upon my lips.
Fate gave us the motive, but left us sick.
Now truth holds out the reasons.
Yet nothing can heal this bleeding spirit...

Left wide open and dry in the sun.
Baking away all that held grace and now it's done.
Soon God will end it and let the credits roll.
But for now we move onward.
Trying to stay warm in this cold...

Reason can't take us any further than here.
Pain may speak the truth, yet it's nothing we'd want to hear.
So now it's passing and leaving behind only remorse.
Nothing can heal this bleeding spirit.
"As no one can save this forsaken ghost."

Humble Whispers

It only matters when you want it to.
It only mattered to me and you.
There was that emotion, now only a stain.
It keeps us in check and leaves us in shame.

Hours left nothing, now it sings through.
Warming our nightmares, and taking our youths.
So there is truly, only those humble whispers.
Holding us, when no one's close.

It makes its way through, and holds us bare.
I once feared it, but now I'm there...
We can't out run it, still it sings its way inside.
The whisper of those memories.
That shall haunt us until we die.

Love – Love?

Still a voice stands out in the dark.
Ten million emotions tearing me apart.
It brings me back, to that last standing day.
Still my heart lays frozen, bleeding acid-rain.

Her kiss as rough as nails against my cheek.
Sliding down and now my eyes begin to bleed.
Passion once held it all "now only pain."
Love meant so much, now just another whim to hate.

Forgiveness was left behind, but never forgot.
Remorse was the name I'd bear, and still I tremble in shock.
Love was once my world, now only a distant star.
My emotions could mean so much.
But they never took me far...

Divine Loathing

Speak no - one last thing and still you wait.
Take no remaining hope and still these bones shake.
Gather all the dust that you can find.
Eat all the ashes, then close your eyes.

Wait ten counts, then let it fall.
Reach into the abyss, to feel nothing at all.
Time can't stop it, only delay its fate.
It seems so divine, your lustful hate...

So reach in a little deeper, take what you can grab.
I've had quite enough, so please end the gab.
Speak no - one last thought and still you wait.
It seems so divine *"your loathing of me..."*

Departed

Will they remember these words when it's done?
Will fate leave a prize, or only dust?
Please answer these questions, before you go.
Please wait a moment and hold me close.

There's nothing more to look forward to.
Now I can only wait for the stars to fade.
Please show me some respect when I leave.
Please give me a kiss that won't wash away...

Dreams may hold us together, but the reality is.
You have left me and I feel much colder.
Somehow or another I can't rest a bit...

Please hold my heart again, before I awake.
Show me some respect as I walk away.
Love me now as I love you.
Remember these words that bind me to you...

No Magic

Go ahead and leave it at that.
Please go away and let me rest.
Take no detour and leave me be.
Let my body rest, and set my mind free...

There's nothing here, left for you.
There is no more compassion, only truth.
Fate and reason now hold the motives.
As pain and anger keep us aware.

There is no more magic left in this body.
I have now only to rest and fade.
There is no more magic left in this soul.
You've taken it all and now I'm drained.

So go ahead and let's call it a day.
Leave me alone and just step away.
There's no more magic left, only grief.
With this last breath, I ask you, please.
"Set this mind free..."

Rain-Fall

Loaded, then we hold hands again.
Frozen, yet we've never forgotten those sins.
Time's waiting, maybe then we could dream.
Now it's loaded, and I can feel it raining on me...

Endless it pulls its way through.
Now all my hopes lie with you.
Forever now and just a little more.
Still I can hear the weeping, from behind the door.

So now it's pouring.
And it seems somewhat a little surreal.
Loaded and she weeps away the feel.
Binding the answers to the rest.
It seems somewhat frozen.
"Her tears and last breath..."

Moving Forward

Can no one hear it ringing in my brain?
Satan tries to help me, yet it'll never change.
Pain was only a word, now the answer I keep.
Love was the connection, now just a sad dream.

Blood was once only a liquid, now my favorite drink.
Time was only a statement, now a demon in me.
Fate tried to take me, but I died instead.
Mother tried to wake me, *"oh, such a sad end..."*

Hatred was only a notion, now it keeps me alive.
Pain was nothing, now a passion of mine.
Miles were taken, now under my feet.
I'm moving forward, and this torment I keep...

Echoing Through

Good morning my love, it's been some time.
Take my hand now, try to open my eyes.
Grip my soul with both hands.
Take this demon and call it human...

Kiss my lips and take the pain.
Grip my tongue and enjoy the taste.
Blackened heartbeats now rushing within.
Can you look inside and see the sins?

Take a note and write it down.
Remember these words and my heart is still unfound.
Now it echoes through, and she weeps.
Tears filling the hole, gaping in my dreams.

Wide awake and she takes my thoughts.
She grips my soul and my body is left in shock.
It echoes through, and she can't wipe away her tears.
As I lay back and let my dreams fade.
So now all my thoughts are gone, yet it's all the same...

No One's Home

Time spoke the riddle, then she turned to ash.
Fate gave me a motive, but I never asked...
Rage was my only companion.
Now reason is driven far, so very far away.
It's like no one seems to care.
So they just throw me away...

Is no one home today?
Am I alone, set here and I just sway.
Is nothing going to change it, the fact of my dismay?
There must be no one home.
Yet still I'm thrown away...

Reality Check

Standing stale and stagnate in the clear.
Pain and anger feasting upon hope and fear.
Day means nothing, and no one's there.
Please wake me now, or take away my air...

So life's a bitch and then we die.
If only it were that easy for you and I.
So death was a joke and now we scream.
Open eyes yet blind, to all the turmoil ahead of me.

Answer the phone, for days now it just rings.
Please show me the end, and let me dream.
Take away my flesh and let the acid rain...
Please give me a new logic-point or let me break.

Anger seems so healthy now.
The poison's growing a little sweet.
Reality was taken, and you stole my last dream.
So open my eyes to the truth inside.
Please answer the phone, or let this subside.

There's no more logic here, only pain and fear.
So life's a bitch and then I died.
Slap me in the face and open my eyes.
Reality no longer has a meaning, yet pain still feels fine.

Chapter 2

Insignificant Other

Sour Plague

Grip my last thought firmly, then let me pass.
Hold my heart, for I am burning.
"I don't really think there will be a happy end."

The acid is flowing and anger growing.
Rage, Wrath, Pain – that's all I've ever had.
So now you're waiting, counting the sand.
So this hour was taken, and never given back.

It tastes so sour - steams over and into my lung.
It seems so tainted, driving me gone...
Insane was a dream then, now my only love.
This plague is my only companion.
It seems so sour as it fills my lungs...

Before the 1st

As the demon spoke the word.
Honor and *Faith* now burn.
Justice raped and left to bleed.
Fate just can't seem to leave us be.

Death was the answer.
So now you take that step.
Anger was a healthy outlet.
Yet now the blood won't wash off the skin.

It meant so much.
Now faded-grim and still she laughs.
It was before the 1st.
When you turned away and never looked back.

Now ashes are filling.
As the demon speaks the last truth.
Justice beaten and screaming.
As *Rage* holds in the last truce.
It was discovered before the 1st.
"A time when all was calm."
Yet as of now we cannot deny.
That our Armageddon comes.

Call Me Sin

It seems so outrageous.
The last-point gone and still you're in shame.
It seems so tainted.
The blister in your heart, and the stain on your grave.
It seems somewhat faded.
Echoing through, and forever it rings over the pain.
It feels so jaded.
So call me Sin, _"for that is my name."_

Breaking the Edge

I sure did love your cynical heart.
It meant so much to me.
Yet now it tears me apart.

I truly did love the taste of the rain.
As acid it fell in, now my brain left stained.
So reason was, and nonsense is...
It's breaking me down, soon nothing will be left.

I sure did love your cynical mind.
It filled me with bliss.
Yet now it's burning me alive.

I truly did love that fact of my dismay.
Yet now it's breaking the edge.
Soon sorrow will be gone.
And only agony shall remain.

I never really did understand your neglect.
I only wished that you would give me a chance.
I truly am grateful for this life.
Yet I seem to only find anger and regret.

I sure did love your cynical heart.
Yet it's breaking the edge.
Now I'm falling apart.

No Hope Left

I want you to do this for me.
I wish I could be there to kiss you good-night.
I want you to just smile please.
Breathe softly and get some rest tonight.

Let nothing stand between you and your goals.
Let no strive label you as weak.
Please just smile, "for me..."

I want you to do this for me.
Take my dreams and set them free.
I want you to be at peace tonight.
Though there may not be any hope left.
"Just smile for me - *alright...*"

Left Out

Frozen rain, still swimming in pain.
Sorrow and sadness, driving my emotions bleak.
Still the clock knows only my dismay.
Forever & Always shall the torment remain...

Take no pity on this lonely soul.
Take no remorse and leave me cold.
Shake my hand and tell me hello.
Kiss your child as I freeze here alone.

The pavement is stemming, red-blood.
The sorrow was leaving, "yet now it floods."
Justice was taken, when you killed my soul.
Honor was broken, now rotting in this hole.

So love your lover and laugh at me.
Kiss your child and watch me scream.
Take no pity on this waste of a man.
Either leave me out, or bury me under the sands...

Now or Never!

Fear holds it always - anger and pain.
I heard the owl calling, somehow it knew my name.
Grace gave me a needle, to place under my eyes.
I just couldn't understand, but now I see the light...

Honor called me a weakling, only to get me to stand.
Now I have a path given, but still I fear the demands.
To compromise on something, I may not want to choose.
It's now or never - to try or to lose...

Spoken

It seems a little strange, yet it's me again.
It took me a little time, to wash clean that sin.
Compassion now jagged, still bringing me close to that.
It was my only weakness, yet I never looked back.

She took my heart, as it was still beating.
She drank the blood, while I was still bleeding.
It was God that was laughing, as I was eaten alive.
It was the Devil that was weeping, as I lost my mind.

It seemed a little shaky, not right in tune.
It felt a little rocky, but now the roses bloom.
God got his laughs in, and the Devil still sobs.
As it was spoken to the endless void, that I'm still alive...

A Hint of Death

Rhyme me a new point of nothing I need.
Sing us a riddle and let the dreamer breathe.
Take note of the torment that I and *you* must mend.
Drink only a sip - before the games begin.

Inhale the last spirit as you kiss my heart.
Take all of what once mattered, then tear it apart.
Love only this notion that I and *you* must un-mend.
Dance through the waking shadows, before it rains again.

Kiss the last failing hope of once you cared.
Take it all and drown it in despair
Rhyme me only a new sort of nonsense today.
Upon you I smell a hint of death.
"It doesn't seem that it will fade..."

It Must Be Something

So there we stand and once again.
So here we go, on and on into a beginning or end.
And so it takes us and no one truly cares.
But she is smiling - now must I prepare?

It could have taken so very much more.
Still the child lies weeping behind the open door.
Fate called the moment, yet no one was home.
Must we battle and battle, straight to the bone?

It must be anger or maybe it's just love.
There must have been a hanging.
"Still I swing, over and above."

All Over Me...

Regret just doesn't seem to cut it today.
Anger was only a thought, now a red stain.
Her smile seems to push me further into the pit.
Somehow or another, *I know this is it...*

She never knew and still doesn't understand.
Now I can feel it waking, from under the dust and ash.
An oddity still standing firm in the frame.
In dirt and grime, forever covered in blood and shame.

Waste deep and over our heads, in the thought.
Regret was the notion, now a fact that will never rot.
It's only an eternity or maybe just our fates.
Covered all over me...
Forever incased in dust, ash, blood and shame.

Vanishing Thoughts

It's a little hazed - gray and weary.
It's a little strange *"can you hear me clearly?"*
Smoke filling the open space, and now I'm alone.
There was once a heart in this chest.
"Now a black stone."

A million nails through my hands and feet.
Thousands of hammers beating down on me.
Timeless torment and so much you don't know.
Endless it pulls and shoves me.
Deeper into this hole...

It's still hazed and weary, *"so can you hear me clearly?"*
The gray pit full, and pain shows only a tried dream.
There was once a human under this skin.
But now that thought is vanishing from me...

Must Be Blind

Humanity is failing, the drug mustn't work anymore.
The bridge is burning, so we jump over and hit the floor.
Rough, as the jagged stones rip away our flesh and dreams.
And we drift away from our faiths, drowning in the stream.

Warmth was waiting, now the blister is torn open.
The blood is flowing, out and into the glass.
It must be - only you and me, *"who knows how this will end."*

Humanity is failing, nerves are torn and wiped away.
The bridge is burning yet the flames are so calming to me.
It must be an ending or the start of a new sort of Hell.
We must be blind *"and for that, humanity shall fail..."*

A Shot of Loneliness

There is this metaphoric face, I seem to hold over the mask.
Some seem not to notice, others are kind enough not to ask.
But it seems as if, no matter how hard I try.
There's always someone out there, waiting to rape my mind.

There is a lie I tell myself, to help get me through the day.
There is this broken shell, which is labeled as my fate.
Yet in the end, summer and winter shall come once more.
No matter how hard I fight it, the truth still waits behind that door...

So I take it, as I wallow deep within myself.
And I hold this metaphoric face over the mask.
"Just to protect my fragile shell."

Now it seems sometimes, as if I'm all alone.
But I know it's true, *"you need only to read the stone..."*
So I take another shot, before the sun halts my rants and faith.
I'd like one more shot of loneliness.
"Before you rape my mind away."

Blue

Love is only a word, yet it's all I have ever truly desired.
Pain is my only companion, that and my faith.
You answered my question.
"Yet it's something I didn't want to hear."
So this rose I hand to you, as I wipe away those tears...

Gripped firm in the hands, of a true symbol of fate.
It is this *"Blue"* feeling that seems to keep me awake.
Never to know, if my heart is healing.
It seems as if it gets worse everyday.

Now you open your eyes and the stars I can see.
Now you kiss my thoughts and haunt my dreams.
How lucky I say, yet I never find sleep.
I would say that I love you.
"Yet this blue-rose, is all I ask you to keep."

My Companion

I think I'm happier with the statement they made.
I know you don't love me, "so let's not play..."
It's just a little lonely - the ghosts packed-up and left.
There's no more ink, for me to write "so I just slit my wrist."

You took my brain-cells and now I freak!
You broke my heart, left me in Hell *"now I'm too weak."*
And you do this, just to get a little attention.
Driving yourself sick, just to get a reaction...

And there's no more actions left for me to choose.
It's come down to this "but I'd rather lose..."
And so you weep it, and let the torments overlap.
I think I'm happier with their statements and facts.

So all the ghosts packed-up and went?
Now I'm all alone, no more voices, just an open stitch.
And my fingers itch, maybe I should just turn out the lights.
So my friend, "blow out the candle and let's end this right..."

Filter-less

Two steps and then it falls.
An angry letter and you lock your jaw.
Unanswered and never censored.
You leave me no choice but to speak.

Timeless it haunts and wants only to know.
As she followed it to the back room.
And waited in darkness, alone.

So light the broken path and let us chant.
Give us another second to end this rant.
Now filter-less thoughts are seeping through.
You can say what you want, but you know it's true.

So let's take our last dive, into the pool of spikes.
Let's swallow it down - maybe with ice.
Now burning our spirits, straight to the core.
Filter-less waiting, as they ask for more...

Suggestion

Head tilted back, gazing up at the wall.
The whiskey rolling down, as smoke still lingers in my lungs.
Neon-purple words seem to show, but maybe it's just a scam.
These eyes could be playing tricks on me.
"Oh God, not again..."

It doesn't make any sense "*so what else is new?*"
You didn't get your rest, and now another memory blooms.
As the eyes gaze up at me, still the purple words loom.
As I smoke away another love.
And drink-down another afternoon.

It's telling me, that I need some help.
Well, I can't deny that fact...
The words are telling me to let it go.
"But I can't breathe, and I'm not coming back..."

99 Bottles

1, 2, 3, 4, 5, 6.
How many more hits will you take?
There they go, against your cheek and across your face.
Slamming you deeper into your dismay.
Rough to the core and straight to the brain.

Gnawing back the lid and you weep.
Eating at the back of your eyes and you freak...
Not taking the time to set it straight.
I'm so sorry but there are those things.
"You just can't change."

1, 2, 3, 4, 5, 6.
How many more hits must you take?
Before you wake-up and realize *"that it wasn't your mistake."*

"Thinking Again..."

Well there you go... "You've got me thinking again."
So are you happy? Now that you've set another whim.
It's not really that funny, yet still we laughed.
It's really not that good, yet not so bad...

And on and on and on and on I go again...
Deeper into the pit called my brain.
How much more ink, must spill from this hand?

Well there you go... "You've got me thinking again."
I hope you're happy, now that the slate is laid.
So here we go, dancing frantic through the rain.
And you must love my pain, or maybe it's just me...

Come to think of it, no one really knows how it goes.
And still you sing along and miss no beat...
I hate you dear and love you so.
Wow, "you really got me to think..."

Futile Dreams

Oh, the pain never seems to subside.
Still the child is asking *why...?*
So has there been another sort of break?
Or are we all, still the very same...?

The smoke is pouring from my every pore.
Still the dream is locked away, behind that door.
So, can no one hear me as I weep here alone?
Still it's futile, dreaming of being home...

When the Record Skips

The pain is the only thing that reminds me, I'm still alive.
The pain is the only thing that reminds me, I'm gonna die...

I'm gonna try, to take the ending and let it be.
I'm gonna cry, as now all the truth of then is behind me.
You'll never try, so now it's waking and breaking through.
I'm gonna die, and let this love-song play for you...

This pain is the only thing that reminds me, I'm still alive.
Your mistake is the only thing that reminds me, we lived a lie.
The song still playing, taking away that one last hope we tried.
When the record skips, it makes you sick.
"So wipe the tears from your eyes."
The pain is the only thing that reminds me, *I'm gonna die...*

If It Were...

Rape my only dream and watch my heart bleed coal.
Take my only want and let the answers scream-cold.
Numb the only reason and now it stands null.
Kiss my lips as you say you love me, and then beat my skull...

So leave it as it was, forever and always untrue.
Now keep my logic and place the horror under that tooth.
Love me now and always until it breaks.
You're more than just an angel, "please forgive my mistakes."

If it were, more than just an ending...
If it were, more than just a second kiss.
If I was, more than just a monster today.
Could you love me, "*if I'm not too late...?*"

Repeat

End the heartbreak of now and before.
Take your last love, locked behind the door.
Bite down onto the moment and watch it spill.
Round and round, and never shall this heal.

Human-meat now growing sweet.
A toxic-lust and a gray-ashy dust.
Filling the endless void known as our souls.
It's breaking on-forth, so soon it will be too cold.

Now shove your arm in and take what's left.
Bite my top lip and taste my breath.
Drive the only pain, known as my heart.
Please tear in once more and break me apart.

"Misery – Misery."

Lovely - and you seem to have so many names.
No shame - and bedtime held so many lies.
Another break - and anger still knows how it goes.
Leave no sympathy, not for this demon - once a man...
"*Oh Misery – Misery...*" Still the world, don't understand.

Hello – Goodbye

Passion seems so distant now that I'm away.
Destruction kind of helps, but the pain never fades.
Hollow, and still the falling star weeps at night.
It sure was great to see you again.
"But I have to say goodbye."

Loaded, and the reason never brings itself forth.
On and on we go again, deep into this endless void.
And it sure did seem so great to see you again.
But only to watch that smile fade, and these dreams break grim.

A smile is all I ask for, that and maybe a laugh...
It sure was great to see you, but now it begins to pass.
Passion seems so distant now that I'm away.
It sure was great, to shake your hand and see your face.

Now hollow in this endless void, I see no escape.
Years and years I've been waiting, but still it's the same.
So numb and cold, as this fallen star weeps at night.
It truly was great to see you again, so "Hello – Goodbye."

No Obsession

I find myself, standing at the bottom of a pit.
Endless as I gaze up, I can see no end.
Forever under these tons of dust and ash.
I'd pull the trigger, but *Death* won't take me back.

There's no more meaning, it's all just a joke.
Again I breathe in, and once more I choke.
So deception never seemed to do the trick.
I find no obsession, as I sway so sick.

Endless as I gaze up, but there's no stars to see.
Only the inside of my skull and rotted dreams.
This cancer is starting to break me down.
You call it my heart, but still I'm un-found.

There are no more hopes left, only dismay.
There are no more smiles, just blood and pain.
There is no happy ending, only funeral-tears.
I have now no obsessions left, "only fear..."

The Last Number

There was a day, when you could count on me.
Now the grave is full, and this dreamer weeps.
Never knowing, and still finding no sleep.

Once more, lost in a prison called my head.
Still rage holds it in, forever till death.
Pain keeps me going, because nothing else works.
Now just one more step out, "*then lock the door...*"

The moment falls down, and time begins to slow.
Rust and lime still hold it, my heart made of coal.
Now sorrow can't change it, but we smile anyway.
Counting down until our number is called.

"*Forever in this purgatory we wait.*"

Reflection-Dim

Wow, it's great to hold you once again.
It's great to know, you've taken away that sin.
It's far out still, lost in the dark.
You're still so amazing *"and my reflection comes apart."*

It's still so sour stinging, salted slits bleeding.
It's gray – gone and leaving, forever left stained.
A one kiss, I never seemed to grasp.
So I gaze into your eyes, and I see my reflection dim.

To: An Old Love

Well, there's not much more to say than that.
A blade left rusted, stuck in my back.
It's been years now, and still you laugh.
I guess it's good to know that you're happy.
I truly am grateful, now that it's passed.

So my statement today, could only be as-such.
I'm so glad that you've forgotten me.
"Now just a moldy book."

Ink still bleeds from there, the hole in my chest.
You'll never give back my heart, but I think it's for the best.
My only true point to make, it leads just passed that mistake.
And still you cut me, *you love to burn me.*
My dear, some things just never change...

It's been so long, far out and under years of dust.
This poison still tastes so sweet.
No one will ever stop this demon that dwells in me.

Well, it's been real but not very fun.
My love, it was great to talk to you once more.
Now this day it must end.
"So if you get the chance to wake me."
"Just slap my mouth once again..."

Chapter 3

Raw Spirits

Flowing Darkness

I love the taste of blood, as it rolls down the back of my throat.
I love the taste of smoke, as I begin to choke.
I love the feel of warmth, but now my body's shaking cold.
I love the pleasure of you and me, but I need to face the fact.
"That this is only a dream."

You lied to me when I needed your trust.
You slapped my face, now my tears - red as blood.
I love the taste of meat, as it's torn from the bone.
I love the feel of security but I have no home.

Come follow me under and throughout the maze.
Creep under your bed, and far inside your head.
Weep if you wish, but no one can stop me...

I love the taste of blood, as it rolls down the back of my throat.
I love the feel of warmth, but now my body's shaking cold.
I've always loved the pleasure of you and me.
But I must face the fact - that you were only a dream...

Miles

Faded dreams and old loves now away.
Pointless tearing, trying to get to the brain.
Mindless wants, and this child knows only loss.
It's still miles away – rusted and locked.

It's been years now, and still she quivers.
It's been so long now, felt only as a sliver.
A hopeless whim of maybe holding love true.
Still it's too far out to grasp, forever now misunderstood.

Rubbed harder against me, now my eyes bleed.
Shoved further within me, beyond the knife I weep.
It stirs up the sorrow, then the rain follows soon.
It's still miles away, forever rusted and locked inside of you...

BackGround

Shouting out in the dark, no one seems to care.
Logic left bitter, spiraling down into despair.
Now anger seems useful, because nothing else works.
"Slaughter would seem helpful, if you weren't already a corpse."
Still they call me bashful, as I'm cast out in the rain.
The world moves on without me, so my sorrow remains.
As it stands in the background, of a picture that everyone can see.
Yet none seem to notice - the ghost in the back was me...

Purple Ash

I can't seem to reason with my mind.
I just can't seem to let a dead love die.
It's pointless now and forever till the end.
It's over now and still we wait for it to begin.

Now the poison rains down, over and into our skin.
The hammer beats down and the blood as sweet as sin.
My heart in a helix, binding and soon to break.
My thoughts are in splinters, so now it's up to faith...

The ashes begin to flutter, kissing your soft cheek.
Now the acid is flowing as my heart begins to beat.
The reasons are still forgotten as was so much more.
And on you wait to see, what stands behind the open door.

Dizzy

It snaps the point back, then the flowers bloom.
The dirt fills the glass, when the angels bring forth doom.
It's spinning faster, soon nothing will make any sense.
Well, I guess we're passed that, so on we fall into the nonsense...
"God wanted a child," to show the word his wrath.
Now I'm a man, "I can never turn back."
Now it's getting harder, to hold myself upright.
Still spinning in circles, as the dust bleeds from my eyes.
I'm sort of dizzy, I just can't find a grip.
It's been years now, "I'm feeling kind of sick."
As the demons maul me, I don't seem to care.
I feel like I'm fading, dizzy-falling-into-fear...

Up-to My Eyes

She called me a handsome person.
Well, I can't really fight with that.
She said I was more than just human.
I enjoyed that - but still don't understand.

Now the spice is rolling over.
Anger left, yet soon to return.
I could bite down onto the edge.
But that might sort of hurt.

So the sunset still waits at the brink.
Still the blood, washes down the sink.
I'm up to my eyes in all of the corpses.
"A flower in one hand and an ax in the other."

It takes some time still, but it might work.
Now I set the drill against my temple, to release some remorse.
I'm up to my eyes in all of the dread.
She called me a great human.
"But they'll never understand."

Wicked Love

An open thought, shut out in the dark.
A lonely child, *freezing-burning* cold in shock.
The storm is rising, bringing on the end.
Soon sorrow will flood, and damnation can begin.

So she kisses my last whim, of maybe and so...
So she takes my heart out, and rubs it with the coals.
Now a lonely bastard, a monster with no fear.
I was once one of God's angels, now I burn in despair.

So it takes some time, to set the records straight.
It's been so long, far out and under the slate.
"So make no mistake, she was mine to keep."
Understand whatever it is you wish to believe.
She stands - my wicked love, burning inside my heart.
Still the emergent thoughts ring inside.
As I wander further into the dark.

Hard Breath

Know me as only a tired waste of frail dreams.
Show me grace, more so than I could perceive.
Give no pity as the blood drips off the moon.
Sing me to sleep, as another *Blue-Rose* blooms.
It hits against my cheek, frozen and then I bleed.
It slams across my head, so say what you want.
"Because I know I am dead."

So it stands-out above all the rest.
Slap my face, because I like that best.
Now this bastard is waiting, and wanting some more.
Drowning myself further, under the floor.
Broken and screaming, as all now decays.
Dripping under the mattress, left forever stained.
Now it steams out of my every pore.
It slams against me, the lost-dream of once before.
Now say what you wish, because I know it's true.
Again it crashes against me, and the blood drips off the moon.

A Nail & a Glass

You couldn't hide it, you could never fight it.
The hours are growing as damnation now fills the open pit.
It takes only a second thought, yet now you rip out the stitch.
So leave it at that, just grope my heart and start the fit.

Take another shot, sleep as it spirals down into your soul.
Beat the child, tear off his skin and leave him in the cold.
Now answer the nothing of when you said you loved me.
Drop that one last hope, so now the hatred is flowing.

Then it springs its way into my brain.
The Devil can keep it, but he couldn't deal with this pain.
I swallow it deeper and laugh as it tears me apart from inside.
It tastes a little sweeter, so warm upon the ice in the glass.
It blisters as it sinks in, beyond the dreams and into the past.

You couldn't hide it, you could never fight it.
Now the child weeps, as his mother rips her own flesh away.
It takes some time to heal the shatter "but you can't hide the shame."
So you take two shots, *a nail and a glass*, lost so deep - in our past.

Innocent Victim

Her words make me feel like I'm drowning.
That voice seems to push me further into the dark.
Her face still makes its way into my brain.
A touch that will forever burn me in my own hell.
It pushed me when I was too overwhelmed.
She knew just how to break me down.
Now I stand as a mound of blood, sweat, paper and ink.
Her words still carry themselves forth.
Onward into the end of all I've ever dreamed.

So she took my hand and gave me that kiss.
My heart fell down, deep in sorrow and the endless abyss.
So I took her voice and pulled it out of my mind.
I never meant to hurt her.
So I locked the door and stand confused.
Now innocence gone and torn away.
Somehow or another her words push me deeper into my grave.
Now we wait hollow and gaze into the pit.
"I truly never meant to hurt my love."
And yet still she gave to me, that one last kiss...

Taste Me Again

Forgive me for all the pains I've inflicted upon you.
Forgive me for all the mistakes I had made with you.
Love me now, forever until the end of dawn.
Please kiss me again while I play your song.

Reach inside and grope my heart once more.
Tear inside to find, it's already behind that door.
Slap my face - because I'm a whore.
Taste me again, for-never more.

Please take my soul and feed it to the dogs.
Molest my body, beat me now - on and on.
Now rape away my only hope of ever seeing tomorrow.
Slit my wrists and throw me into the hollow.

So God please forgive me for all my sins.
Forgive me for my mistake that broke your heart.
Please give me the chance to burn for you.
Please taste me again, then lock my tomb...

Skull

Now darkness drips off and into your mouth.
The insects pulse as the dead-meat is pulled out.
It festers inside until the day you understand.
Still my body - can't meet your demands.
I think something's happened, the clouds now fall.
I think someone's out there, waiting under the frost.
Still you call it nonsense as I dig deeper inside.
I beat and crack it, and spill out my life.

It takes its toll now, today marks the day.
Now you can relax, soon this monster will be put away.
So I beat it harder, and watch it spill onto the concrete.
It boils and cooks on this hot summer day.
So darkness now fills it, the open hole in the back.
I pushed and shoved it, so now you can relax.
The insects eat it, all my knowledge spilt onto the ground.
Now darkness drips into my skull, as blood pours from my mouth.

A Demon Named "Me."

A hot spike is shoved through both my eyes.
As I lie down and bleed, I again wonder why.
There is no meaning to this torment I endure.
So why must you beat me and lock the open door?
They all hate me because I have a mind.
I know you hate me, please don't waste my time.
So now it's over but yet to even begin.
So now I'm dead and waiting for this to end.

I'm nailed tight against a wall, knives and needles in my skull.
So I'm the most hated for just being myself.
As I wait here alone in my own hell.
I know I'm shattered, "you laughed when I fell."
So I'm the one who is feared, again the children throw stones at me.
I'm the monster in the clear, that's why they burned me.
I was just an innocent child of God.
Now I wander alone in darkness, frozen forever in frost.
They all hate the demon named "Me."
Yet I've asked nothing more than to be free.
I was once a human, yet they burnt out my eyes.
Now I am a demon, for the world to despise.

The Worm

It slimes its way through all the fears of this child.
It makes its home in the back of my head.
It eats at all my hopes and dreams.
Soon it'll take control, and nothing will be left of me.

Now my body's failing, soon just a black-ash.
My mind is breaking, it's taking all of what I had.
Will nothing stop this monster that's eating my soul?
Please kill me now, before it takes control...

Will no one save me, am I all alone?
It's so dark now, so very – very cold.
The worm is feasting on all of who I was.
Soon I'll be nothing more than a shallow pool of blood.

Please end this torment of the parasite inside.
Will nothing end this burning pain at night?
Please stop this worm that's feasting on my soul.
God please! "Kill me now, before it takes control."

Infest

Through my eyes, can you see?
A million monsters, a thousand demons infesting me.
They take their time and do it right.
My body now decaying from far inside.

They run through my veins and break my heart.
They speak through my voice and rip us apart.
Now they rule me and tell my thoughts to burn and die.
They lift the pistol, then place it against my eye.

Soon it'll be over and nothing more than a stain.
Still they break me, now my heart insane.
So nothing can save me, and no one will.
Still they infest me, as I lay under this hill.

They tear my conscious and destroy my will.
A million monsters inside me. A thousand demons from hell.
Still no one can save me, as they control my head.
I can scream if I wish, but soon I'll be empty and nothing will be left.

Chew Me Harder

It's a little sweeter today, so get your fill.
It's a little hard to scream, under the ash and filth.
So reach in deep and take what's left of me.
Tear open the hole and laugh as I weep.

Bite down harder and strike me again today.
Pull out my tongue and sing the song for me.
So you laugh at the slaughter, of this child named *Sin.*
Chew me harder, as the blood rains down again.

It tastes a little sour, because I was left out too long.
It tastes a little bitter, so eat me while I'm raw.
It tastes a little flushed, so add some sugar and lime.
Chew me harder and leave nothing left but the acid of my spine.

Lust & Rust

It's a little hard, when I don't use those words.
"You took it a little far..."
When you held me down and licked my scars.
Now pain is gone, yet the only thing here.
The needles hold in the frantic-memory, now all alone in fear.
So kiss my left eye, to see how all of this will end.
Pull out my back tooth, and burn the bloody skin.
Reach into the lost ages of when no one cared who I am.
Lick the back of my ear, sing me to sleep once again.

Now tied to the bottom of the deepest pit called hell.
As all the lingering notions break so overwhelmed.
Love me now and shove the knife into my spine.
It's a little hard, now that you've taken it too far.
Rubbing my skin away with the blade of the ax.

Please sit back and try to relax...
It's just a little hard to say, when I don't use those words.
You took it too far today, when you laughed as I burned.
Now you pull the chains through my flesh, and I scream.
You feel a quiver between your legs as I weep.
Now pain is gone, as is all that ever held me dear.
You get your kicks from this lust and rust.
Dwelling forever in my fears...

Whiplash!

It snaps it back, when all the hopes beat against the front.
It takes its time, as blood fills both lungs.
Now memories are forsaken, as is this child of sin.
It rips it all back, throwing us to the front once again.

Soon pain will rule, when sight comes back.
Now the middle is torn, open and at such a lack.
The passion has spilt, out and into the hollow.
It takes us back once again, snapping it as the anger follows.

It takes some time still, but now you can no longer stand.
It's broken out of place, "will no one understand?"
So now it's over, but pain rages on.
It snaps us back, as we're thrown to the front...

Call It 2-Side

A loveless life leading anger, up-down - over and through.
An old emotion fleeting, leaving only fear and pain.
A comma stuck between, now sorrow begins to drain.
It finds its way through, then makes its home inside.
That old whim still lingers, *Round-inside* - the deepest part of my head.

This anger still building, on and on until the end.
Love left bleeding, a wounded child alone in bed.
Emotions left frozen, until someone takes my hand.
Endless it piles up, as the years fade with the sand.
Here it's held firm, buried under the tears and ash.

Someone called me a demon and now the world burns me dead.
Somehow I lost all the meaning, when she turned away her head.
Now murder seems sweeter, but somehow I clear my mind.
Still I stand between, and again I step over the line.

So now it's come down to faith, so I guess I'm out of luck.
And now it's a broken slate, six feet under the mud.
And still they call me a bastard, but I know it's true.
So it's only this comma that stands between me and you.
Still it's dark, as anger and sorrow bleed down the drain.
Left so far in the back of my mind.
Someone please tell me, what to call this emotion inside..?

Upchuck

There it goes, now the world knows what's inside.
So there you go, just wipe the tears from your eyes.
And now it's flowing and filling the open pit.
So now it's frozen, and I soon won't forget.

There's nothing to stop it, and no one will.
It's spreading across the canvas, as I hide in my lonely shell.
Because no one wants me, the demon-child now awake.
No one can save you, so make your peace and clean the slate.

It moves up further because I know what it's for.
It falls into the shadow and spreads across the floor.
So now it's showing and everyone can see.
Now it's flowing, as I watch the child scream.

Steaming

An angry life still leading to pain.
Darkness still flowing, rushing through my brain.
It fills the opening and then no one seems to care.
I'm still your child, alone and out of air.

And then it breaks the point and no one can see.
As all that once mattered now burns inside of me.
Because no one seems to notice when my flesh falls off.
Now the backwards-emotion is steaming.
"Soon humanity will be lost."

So now it's down to faith, and again I fail.
As it steams through my eyes, because I'm already in hell.
Anger seems so helpful, but you're already dead.
I can never melt the snow, so I guess this should go unsaid.

And darkness forever drips down into the empty pit.
I don't know if it will ever be filled.
"So maybe I should just quit."
But rage still seems to be the only one on my side.
As all the hatred is still steaming.
And another leaf bleeds from my eye.

Maggot-Mass

There it goes, now they're falling out of my mouth.
Into the dirt, as they bathe in my sweat and blood.
It fills the space, the smell of rotting meat and dread.
The cool chill now rushing down to my feet.
It drives all the memories gone, now too weak.

Because fate never seemed to take me far enough.
Now the decay is all that can satisfy the maggot-rush.
And it makes me feel flushed, so very-very cold and crushed.
Yet still it pushes, as they eat their way out of my skull.
What can I say now? It's too damn cold.

So there it goes, now they're falling out and into the glass.
Still they eat my heart and tear away my past.
Soon sorrow will remain and nothing more.
This maggot-mass takes control, soon the blood will freeze.
And there's no stopping it now, because you're still too weak.

Spilt Over

Nothing now and still the open door breaks the trend.
It's over now so take off your noose and let us in.
So it's waking now and your eyes know only sin.
It's a backwards hate but no one will tell you more.
It's almost great, but still a worthless whore.

Now hatred is steaming and seeming to know no end.
Lust was a great pastime but now I'm alone again...
So rip apart my last hope of seeing another day.
Dig it deep and pour the acid into my hollow grave.

Just hate my existence and kill me once more.
And again these words spill over, out and onto the floor.
And no one opens the door, so let's leave it locked.
The stain means nothing, so let's please just end this talk.

My spine can't hold this, the pressure building until a break.
Please end the drilling, just pull the trigger and take my brain.
So now it's waking, since it spilt over and into the hollow.
Still hatred is steaming, breaking the memory of tomorrow.

Slap! Slap! Gone...

It seemed real nice, until she put out the cigarette on my eye.
It seemed real great, until she slit my wrist in rage and hate.
Now passion has passed and only fury remains.
She took me so far and left me standing in the rain.

So it seemed real fitting for the mood that day.
A blood-red moon and my lungs forever stained.
Now hate is all that loves me, so love is all I hate.
It still kind of gets to me, but I fixed my mistake.

So then it slammed against me, her fist across my face.
Then I awoke to the nightmare, known as my life and fate.
So nothing now comforts me, only the chill of death.
It seemed real nice when she loved me, but now she's dead.

So anger never helped it, but it's so damn funny to me.
The slap across my face, as I stood there doing nothing.
But then the memory reminds me, that I'm still just a freak.
I have nothing more now, just *Slap! Slap! Gone...*
And now truth is forever stained upon me.

Made of Meat

It falls down breaking, straight to the bone.
The screaming shadows waking, someone take me home.
Now mother is leaving and no one's there.
The dizzy pills falling, soon – no more air...
Please someone care, and tell me I'm more than just me.
Please make sense of this pain and let tomorrow ring.
Because nothing is helping and no one will.
It falls straight to the bone and takes me to hell.

I'm nothing now, just a sad little side-show freak.
I'm no one today, because you stole my identity.
Now the reasons are torn and nothing can mend.
Now it's all just a lie, as is this feeble skin.
So I'm made of meat and pointless dreams.
So I'm just a corpse, waiting to set myself free.
And nothing will end this and no one's there.
Now mother is leaving and I'm out of air...

Deterioration

Grounded and now it steams inside my fears.
Unannounced and now it hides behind the tears.
Your hatred for me, can only prove to be the just cause.
Nothing can save me now "nothing at all..."

Just leave my heart out and let the insects infest.
Take my hollow dream and leave nothing left.
Now I'm a forsaken man, waiting to be something more.
But nothing can save me now, never – never more...

Just pointless now, so I lock the feel.
It's all just a backwards-dream, as I lie beneath this hill.
And no one will help me, but still I scream at night.
Grounded to all that I once thought was real.
So now I weep as I lie infested beneath this hill...

Can't Beat Original

Again I stand and watch my hopes fall.
Again I wander, further into the dark and behind the wall.
It's so cold inside yet only hell's fire burns.
It's so lonely out here, and I've still yet to learn.
So nothing can change it, the memory of then.
No one can save it, the angel in dread.
And again the torment files, so deep inside my head.
Once more I wake up, to realize I'm already dead.
You can't beat me today, not at my own game.
You can't take my soul, because I'm already cold...
This nightmare still haunts me, but again I'm awake.
You can't kill this monster that dwells within your mistakes.
They never understood my screaming, as I wept all alone.
They could never end the dreaming, so please just clear the stone.
Because you can't save this demon, "no you can't correct this lie."
You cannot stop this ticking time bomb, so just close your eyes.
And again I stand just to watch my dreams fail.
"No one can save me, and no one will."
It's so cold in this grave now, I'm weeping all alone.
You can't beat me any longer, I have no soul.
You can't take my pride, because that's all I have.
You can't beat original, and you'll never understand...

Her Toxin

It seeped so deep behind my eyes. It took me far and left me to die.
Now revenge is held, as I stand here screaming.
Now she's alone, "can you hear her weeping?"
Behind the moon and over so many drinks.
It was her-toxin I took and now my soul sinks.
Into the *Never* and so very far away. I tried to save her but she just walked away.
The devil can take this emotion, but I'm already there.
Shoved deep under the headstone and behind so many tears.
Now passion was left somewhere, but I just don't know.
I took her-toxin and now I'm all alone.

Soul-Decay

It's burning and burning, but I cannot just end this.
It's hating and waiting, for someone to free it.
I'm not there, just somewhere of no care, just hollow.
It's leaning and gleaming, over the shadow.
Now hollow, I'm hollow and waiting for sorrow.
Please wake me, just hate me, *God I cannot just take this...*

Some fear – now clear, as all the pain just fades inside.
No fear – while I'm here, standing over the cradle.
Now tear – why there? Please give me some pity now.

It's waiting and hanging, over the hallow.
You shamed me, you hate me, now taking, me hostage.
Inside the – the empty, of leaving me under.
It's dying, decaying - now the sorrow it's steaming.
It's over, I'm over, just leave me for someone.
It's burning, I'm burning, but no one can end this...

Some fear – not clear, as all the pain still builds inside.
No care – while I'm there, "place the thorn into my eye."
Now tear – why there? Please tell me it's okay now...

It's over, I'm over, just waiting for credits.
It's shallow, so hollow, but seems so – so hallow...
You're running, still running, fighting for reason.
It's dying, decaying, and waiting for reason.
No reason, for reason, you're *leaving* for someone.
Decaying, I'm burning, still burning, but no I cannot just end this.

Raw

Take me back, to the day I realized I was awake.
Take me back, to the shallow pool of liquid hate.
Take me further than this Hell called my human mind.
Take me home now and sing me another rhyme.

So end the torment of the flesh that still hangs on.
Rip my face off and cover me with lime.
Now torture seems, so distant today.
Just rub me raw and eat away my face...

It's such a waste to me, so knock me off my feet.
Drink the steam, as my blisters bleed.
It's such a down-shove, of a lonely fantasy.
It's not what I asked for, but it's still a suicidal feat.

So take me back, to the day I woke up in Hell.
Take me back, to the dark pit under the empty well.
Take me further than this existence of human skin and dust.
Take me now, so we can beat the rush...

Just end this torment, of what stood at the end of the hall.
Drink my soul away and eat me while I'm raw.
Collapse my conscious and laugh as God burns me again.
Take me while I'm raw, and cover yourself in the blood from off my skin...

Chapter 4

The Shortest Straw

Full of It

A deeper point to be made, when no one seems to care.
Now all that was said, just fades with despair.
It means nothing to you, but still you sob.
It was all for a reason, but now it's lost.
A bitter noise that still rings behind my teeth.
Her shallow voice that still tries to scream.
It means nothing to me, so just take a breath.
You mean nothing to me, so let's end this stress.

It's a deeper point to be made, but no one's there.
It's a little hard to be saved, when no one cares.
Now only this hollow shell, stands between me and fate.
And still she tried to scream, far under the slate.
It's no wonder that you still weep yourself to sleep.
It's such a bother, as were you and me.
Now the steam rises off the blood, but no one seems to flinch.
You still try to make your point "but I know you're full of it..."

In - A Little Deeper

Clear the stage please, and let the monster dream.
End the demonic screams, just watch as the skin melts away.
Take my lonely wish of when I was not so alone.
Rip my heart into pieces, and fill this endless hole.

Grip my eyes in your hands and let me cry today.
Reach in - a little deeper so you can take it all away.
And now it's all just a story that no one wants to read.
Now my life is just a memory that no one wants to keep.

It goes so much further but no one will see.
It means so much, now that you don't believe.
I could answer all the questions, but no one ever asks.
I could be a man of faith, but I never looked back...

Please clear all these nightmares out of my troubled skull.
Take what was once valued and burn it with the coals.
"Just a charred outline that everyone overlooks."
Reach in - a little deeper and take my heart of soot.

And the Rain

You left when no one would believe.
Now all stands hollow and forever behind the rhyme.
You took it all from me.
So now I'm weeping till my heart's forever dry.
It meant so much to me.
But no one lets me hold it close and enjoy the light.

You broke all my wants and faith.
Now my soul stands hollow and covered so deep in shame.
You stole my youth and my only dream.
Now and forever I lie awake and drown in my screams.
It hurts so much to know you're still alive.
Forever now the blood drains from both eyes.

It meant so much but you don't care.
You loved me to death but now we're there...
So cold as the sorrow steams off the knife.
And the rain can't wash off the stain.
So now and always, I lie awake - screaming all night...

She Laughed

Millions of stars dancing overhead.
So cold that night, "the day that was best left unsaid."
But still it haunts me, the words that forever ring.
Still it plagues me, the open door and endless screams.

It was a good try at best, but who am I now?
It was a great lesson to learn, but I didn't know how.
So I stand here dreaming, wishing I could rip out my spine.
I lay here weeping, soon I won't remember why.

It was raining that day, so very – very cold.
The chill ran so far within, freezing me numb to my soul.
I tried to make a difference, "*but I guess I did...*"
I tried to show that I loved her, yet now it's an open stitch.

Millions of stars, dancing over head.
It was cold that night, and still I can't shake the dread.
It was very moving to me, but no one else cared.
She just laughed as I walked away, "*wandering deeper into nowhere.*"

Make It Rest!

My name, it's lost upon a stage.
Forever-through, and beyond the rage.
It took me far, yet nowhere fast.
Still tormented and losing my past.
It makes no sense, to eat my heart.
It's empty now, and made of tar.
You laugh at my worries but still I weep.
Please end the nightmares and let me sleep.

It tastes so sweet and sour nails.
Biting and tearing, me into hell.
So make it rest and go away.
Please find my identity, upon that stage.
Forever-through, and beyond my rage.

Spit My Voice

Far over the viewpoint, that you call faith.
Way under the radar and further passed those mistakes.
She calls herself an angel, because I'm just a beast.
So I can only smile, as they tear the bone from meat.

And they laugh it full, of only spite.
When I turn away and close my eyes.
Because nothing heals it, the shattered skin.
And no one can forgive it, my eternal sin.

It takes so much of me, when I spit out my voice for you.
Now I can only remember, the time when I had killed myself for you.
Under all the views, of a justice so blind.
Still they call us "free," as we're lined-up like swine.
We are just pointless lies, with flesh draped over.
And now it all pours, as I spit out my voice for you.

Out for You

A scream beyond the bleeding child.
Forty more lines and one last push towards denial.
A shattered emotion, when all the little things are gone.
So now you're just a memory, just a forgotten love-song.

You swing it so clearly above all, that means more today.
And all those years must have been, just another bad daze.
So you leave the worries, of a child left in a hole.
You pay it no mind, as he freezes under the snow.

It's taking us further and over the edge.
Someday we'll hit, and I'll wake-up dead...
For not once-ever, yet still she laughs at the pain.
So now this monster is out for you.
Never to show mercy or let-up the bane.

Judge Me Again

So you take my face and begin to erase it.
You take my faith and label me as a heretic.
So why am I not what you wish me to be?
Should I go back to church to make God listen to me?

I'm just a demon with words, and no one even cares.
Yet for some reason or another, I'm still drowning in despair.
Taken by my wrist, and beaten with a cross.
So now I just laugh, as you pull my skin off.

Lord please hear me and shut the Hell up!
And I will not say I'm sorry, nor forgive that slut.
Yet you judge me again and take all my dreams.
But someday I'll escape from this hollow eternity.

I'll make my way through the crowd of sheep.
I'm just a heretic with another hallow dream.
And you judge me again because I'm not your reflection.
So should I stand up once again, to teach you a lesson...?

Cure the Hate

Please cure this hate and let me love once more.
Please take me away and unlock the door.
Let passion break through and give us a motive.
Please call me a human and clean off my headstone.

Cure all the sicknesses that infest my body.
Kill all the demons that scream so late at night.
Take all that once stood for truth and justice.
Break them down and sell them for pennies.

Rage once helped it but now you're gone.
I would just sit back and relax, but now I feel the twitch.
The haze lingers over as all the lights begin to dim.
I wake up and you're on the floor, and it's red.
Please keep it loaded, so you can cure the hate and sin...

The Road of Choice

I once spoke those words when I was young and naïve.
Now the match still burns but can't last an entirety.
Still her voice rings on, in the back of my head.
But now it's just another, hollow-whisper of dread.
I once felt the sharp push on the back of my spine.
Then I turned, and stopped the emotion on a dime.
I looked her in the eyes and knew that it was over.
So I've known all along, of the inevitable outcome.

A push so far and over but now it rings clear.
The silent whisper that still carries on through the years.
A point once made and a logic that's forever just.
A path lain out for me and this demon under the dust.

It's a bold fact and most call it cruel.
It was a long road and so much more I've yet to observe.
I might be half way there or just at the start.
I know not where this story ends, "maybe above the stars."
But the one thing I've come to know through all of this.
I will die alone and lie forever in the abyss.
I spoke those words once, when I was young and naïve.
Now I step forward, on this path I chose for me.

A Shadow With a Name

The points are fading, yet somehow I stay strong.
The pages are burning, soon we'll eat the ashes with salt.
The faces are gone now, wiped away over the years.
So now they're just demons with distorted flesh.
Unable to shed a single tear.

The bones are healing but still stuck out of the skin.
The words are still echoing, but can't move us again.
We can't hold on much longer, under these years of mold.
Soon we'll forget each-other and leave this story un-told.

It's breaking faster and only Death smiles through this.
God can't hear us from here "no point in slitting our wrists."
The Devil can't save us today - now we understand the test.
It's taking too long, to end this nightmare of yesterday.
So who am I now? Just a shadow with a name...

Break It

Father - Can you hear me as I scream from under the ice?
Mother - Please smile today and close my eyes.
Take the time for a while and let me see once again.
Lie to me once more, to shelter me from this world of sin.
Take all that was once my body and burn it now.
Spread my ashes over her grave, just to watch her shout...

Father – Can no one save this soul of rage?
Mother – Why are the needles still causing me pain?
Please end the dream of a better lie to be said.
Burn me now, so I can wake up dead...
Let's call it a compromise or just another page.
Break my heart once more, before I go insane.

My brother and sisters don't know of this monster inside.
All my friends tried to help, right before they died.
So now I'm screaming, as my love still doesn't exist.
Please break it all, my body and soul - my heart and spirit...

Sooner

A darker dream, beyond all the faded hopes.
Another scream, under the years of mold.
Pointless breaks and another bloody ax.
Endless pulling, the blade from my back.

Angels falling, burning alive.
Demons feasting, as we rip out our eyes.
She calls me a mistake, just a hollow dream.
I've had enough of this war, so I'll let out some steam.

The end is sooner, closer than you could know.
The monster's alive now, yet still under the snow.
Those hammers beat it, and drive me away.
I'll find you sooner or later, so you better stay awake.

Remaining Hug

I can't describe that feeling.
Of the angel that holds me together.
I still feel it stabbing,
But it can't go on forever.

The pills are dragging me down.
Further into the decay of nature.
The worms are getting bigger.
Crawling through my veins.
I can't love the Devil today.
So please cover our graves.

I can't describe that feeling.
The hug that remains through the wrath.
Yet I can still feel her stabbing.
As my memories turn to ash.

A Kiss of Ash

A lie once told just to make me feel better.
It was a rusted chain, now holding me together.
It was only a white-lie, so I wouldn't get hurt.
It was all for a reason, but now those memories burn.

Under miles of heartbreak and so much unsaid.
Further than any demon could come to know.
Festering so soundly under the tears and smoke.

Now waking sooner, before the child sees.
Another stone pulled through and the wound still bleeds.
A line before breakfast and now you know.
It was only a lie you said, beyond all the smoke.

Just a lonely nail beaten further inside.
The chain still holds me, until the day I subside.
It was only a simple tale you said, to keep me safe.
You gave only a kiss of ash, now my heart's forever stained.

Dire Mechanics

More than just a better year to be spent.
No more alcohol left to clean off our skin.
Faces pushing through all the pages of my fate.
All the gears are turning, but these emotions never change.

Grinding down and now the summer seems to fade.
Another laugh, as all the angels remember my mistake.
So should I have listened to myself from the start?
It's too close to the end now, we can see only stars...

Busted lower than the furthest pit of hell.
It was more than just a smile, but now overwhelmed.
All the pieces of the puzzle seem to hold me together.
The gears begin to tighten, gripping everything inside.
It was more than just a sad ending - more than just a bitter lie.

It was all but dire mechanics, of the everything that makes me who I am today.
There is no alcohol to clean off these wounds, still forever-stained.
The faces push through, all that divides me from them.
The gears still turn on and on, moving me further into my own head...

Sheltered Skin

Whipping flames, ripping away all that was once my heart.
A shallow grave, just so I can gaze up at the stars.
A nail shoved through, but that was years ago.
Another weeping demon, chewing at the stone.

There was once a girl that thought that she could help it.
A bitch that knew she would get hers in the end.
It's been years since I've died.
Yet I'm still waiting for it to begin.

The worms eat at it, so I guess I have no eyes.
Still the needles fall in, deep into my spine.
You hold me inside, trying to taste where I've been.
So I bathe in these flames, just to shelter my skin.

Fever

It boils inside, taking me closer to fate.
The white lights are dimming.
So I guess that's what I get, for making mistakes.
And Jesus would love to guide me.
But what can I do when I'm blind?
My body's getting hotter "I think I'm gonna die..."

There's a lot I've meant to say over the years.
But I could never seem to find the time.
Now the sands are flowing faster.
Soon gone and you'll turn off the lights.

This fever, it's making me forget your voice.
All that I once loved about you, now *null and void*.
But in the end, the dirt you throw over me won't be clean.
But what would you expect "remember – it's Me..."

My eyes are blurred and my head's on fire.
There is no saving me now, so please just smile.
Take all the time you have, to laugh at this wasted mistake.
This fever has taken control, so I guess I won't awake.
My eyelids are heavy, I'm sorry I didn't get to say goodbye.
Jesus – what the hell am I going to do?
"I think I'm gonna die..."

Opening My Eyes

Sand rubbed against, soon I'll be blind.
Another worm feasts, hidden within the lime.
It makes no sense to you, because you never cared.
The dream is almost over, but now I'm out of air...
So open my eyes and tell me that it all matters.
Grab my heart and head, quick – before it splatters.
And now the chatter is overflowing at the end of the hall.
Can you hear the little demons, weeping behind the walls?

The pain rushes through, then the tea washes it all away.
Please open my eyes so I can see the mistakes.
Let all this torment, mean something more in the end.
As I try to find a meaning, as to why I woke up again...
It rubs against me, the broken glass in my throat.
The smoke feels heavy, yet I never seem to choke.
All the emotions begin to rob me.
Of anything that you could call humanity.
But now I'm opening my eyes, and I can see no more sanity.

Sober

So it's pulled and the mask holds no grain.
So I'm a fool, lingering over those past mistakes.
A bitter man wishing he could pull the trigger.
A hollow soul knowing there's no bullets.

Frozen and now the shock begins to sink in.
It slams against me, and now the storm begins to shift.
Bleeding rain, falling over the beach of a child now lost.
Reality was a good idea but God must have forgot...

The pens are beginning to rust inside.
It's a shallow pool but please – give it time.
Waste not what you call my reflection today.
Just salt your drink, with the dust of my grave.

I'm all alone in this vice-driven sanitarium.
Trying to find another bitter-irony to rhyme.
I'm breaking down in my sobriety.
Sober-screaming as the shock eats my reality alive.

Where I'm Going

I owned the world, once upon a time.
Now I'm just another insect, eating the dirt and grime.
Nothing makes sense to me now.
I wish I could reach you, but now I'm fazed-out.

So that's my luck, I guess it could be worse.
So now I'm stuck, falling deeper into this page.
No one can save me now and no one gives the time of day.
So I think I'll take that last step, into the morning haze.

It's all, just another tormented scream for me to seep.
I'm heading further into the back of my mind, where no one will see.
I need to escape this monster that's eating me inside.
I wish I could tell you where I'm going.
But I don't think you'd give me the time...

When You Smile

The ground crumbles away when the tide comes in.
It all falls inside, the purple-clouds bring the ghosts to life.
It tickles my heart, when I remember *"I don't have one..."*
The voices ring hollow, echoes dripping down my spine.

So it takes me awhile to pull myself together.
I know you laughed when I shattered under the rain.
Your melody still holds me, but *"I can't hear a thing..."*
It means so much to me, now that you don't mean a thing.

The world begins to crumble under my feet when you smile.
The stars rip my flesh away, with the forgotten poems of then.
I know you were there that day, *"the last one held..."*
I felt so warm when you smiled, but I was the one who failed.

Flowing under, as the tide slowly takes me away.
I watch the earth melt and then I remember, you took my eyes away.
My memories fade, and then I know that you were here.
I love it so much when you smile.
But then again I remember, *"that you're not there..."*

Under the Page

It was years ago, now buried beneath the smoke.
A feeling of all the demons that dwell inside.
Now what am I going to do with this blade and rage?
What was the meaning, when you had licked at the bloodstain?

Locked forever in this rusted cage.
Those words must mean something, "but nothing will ever change."
Sometimes it feels as if the blood won't drain.
But I know the answers lie forever, under the page.

Etched so deep, into the middle of my forehead.
I can't live on, in this cage made of skin.
It feels like it was years ago, now just faded in the smoke.
But somehow I still feel it deep inside.
I know not why it is you had left that bloodstain.
But I know that the truth waits forever, under the page.

Ancient History

The paint can't hold it forever - though we try.
The ink won't save a memory, just give it time.
The wax holds it over, trying to mean something more.
The blood spells out the logic, but you locked that door.

The bones and dust cradle those dreams of you and I.
I wish I could forget you, the reflection of my mind.
It's all nailed tight, and then the ages mold us as one.
The artwork won't last forever, but still we try.

It's all ancient history, the name of her and me.
This story is already over, but still I write – you read...
Nothing stands between us, only ash and mold.
The centuries of blood and mayhem – disorder and decay.

The picture keeps us open to the facts of fantasy.
The ink can only flow for so long, now dried-out and history.
I know it's grim, but the wax can't preserve us forever.
So we age on in this story, fading deeper into the page.
The paint won't last forever "but still you hold onto this frame."

A Failing Dream

As I cut myself open, only dust bleeds out.
It's all just numb weeping, as I scream and shout.
There are no more angels or dragons left to keep it going.
There are no more monsters under the bed.
I would so enjoy the torment of being forgotten.
But I've already been dead.

The leaves turn black, and I know that sound.
All we once feared it as children, now it keeps us down.
Held against the rotten door.
Screaming, crying but still only a corpse.

So soundly driven, a lie we live still – today.
Only ashes bleed from my open wounds.
A numb tear rolling down my face.
I would so enjoy watching you burn me again today.
But once more I remember - I'm already in my grave.

Cross My Path

Rage pulls through, the reason for another day.
The pain feels smooth, because you like it that way.
So here I am - a Sadist in a Masochist's world.
A lonely fool, watching my photo albums burn.

It's all for a reason, or maybe I just don't care.
I'm just another bad dream.
"A monster for your children to fear."
The last number called, I guess I got the shortest straw.
Just sitting alone here, awaiting the rain...

So cross my path and step barefooted over the broken mirror.
Watch the years fade and go, just another salty tear.
It flows through and I enjoy all this rage.
So I slap you again, and you ask another – "please..."

The skin feels dry, or maybe it's just the ground.
This heart won't beat, forever it's unfound.
So cross me again and let's see if you'll survive.
I love hurting you and you take it all with a smile...

One Inch Deeper

Do it slow – take your time as you drive the blade in.
Bite my ear – whisper those words I want to hear.
Rip it smooth – then tear it all from one end to the other.
It's almost there – just take your time and do it right.

The colors no longer reflect in these eyes.
You sang me a song but you wasted your time.
The cradle broke and then I fell.
You wouldn't catch me, so now I'm in Hell.

The roach inside, it eats all my dreams.
I'm nothing to you now, just a tragic dream.
Please forget me if you can, burn me away.
Do what you do best, and leave me in my grave.

So do it slow – take your time as you drive the blade in.
Bite my ear – cloud all my memories with pain and fear.
Rip it smooth – the blade can almost reach my heart.
So go on and push it, one inch deeper and I'm torn apart.

What I Am

There in the back, nothing blankets the dread.
Once upon a time we smiled but now those emotions are dead.
The frame holds the reason but *truth* is just a lie.
We all know what it takes to make a monster.
"So why did you try?"

Laid under the slate and forgotten before you knew my name.
What was I back then and who am I today?
"Just a freak, eating away the unjust."
Or am I a holy man – ash to ash, and dust to dust...

So what was the meaning? Now my flesh won't grow back.
The hallow-ground is steaming, now I'm off track.
Unforgiven for the action, of destroying my immortal soul.
What am I – just a dead child hidden behind the coals...

Because of You

I remember a time, when tomorrow didn't matter.
I remember a day, when all I wanted was a smile.
Now it's blurred and nothing makes any sense.
It was all for her but now I drown in all my sins.

My face no longer means anything to God.
My faith was tested and I think I lost.
There's no one to blame for my mistakes but me.
But I sold my soul because of you. *So now I'm just an empty sheet.*

Torn edges and nothing can mend this shattered shell.
I'm full of needles and ink. So I sink to the bottom of the well.
Lightless weeping no tears from my rusted eyes.
I did this all because of you "so I think I deserve that smile..."

On The Other Side of Me

So you're the reflection I've aspired to gain.
The answer, as to why I bother to breathe.
You're the outcome I've fought to gain.
You're what I've desired all along.
The cure to all of my pains.

The tide is gone with me, and now I'm under the stars.
There must be a reason as to why I care.
Maybe I still have a heart...

The frozen blade can't keep the door locked forever.
We all know how this man will end today.
Maybe I'll close my eyes for only a moment.
Or I could just drink all the spirits away.

You're the answer as to why I'm standing here alive.
You were the one that kept me going.
"The one light that shined through the fright."
A better motive for me to believe in, a new logic for me to try.

You are the reflection I've aspired to gain.
"The reason that I woke-up today."
You are the one that gave me a better reason to breathe.
The one who stands - on the other side of Me.

Chapter 5

Who Gives a Damn?

Controlled Chaos

So many steps onward, into the pointless push.
Trying to give reasons and purpose for all the battles we took.
But no one goes home with honor and pride.
Just endless nights of screams that never seem to die.

We fight so hard to give meaning to this futile war.
We try to label our disputes with Grace, like the ones before.
They've created a notion that men and women strive for.
A single thought that millions have died for.

The children weep under the flags soaked in blood.
Crying out for the sun to dry this horrific mud.
So their children can tell their children.
That there was a purpose to all the mayhem.

They say we fought for peace and justice.
"And we'll fight again and again..."
But in the end, peace is just another word.
We fight and die more and more.

"We must find *Controlled Chaos*.
If ever we're to end our wars..."

Saving Yesterday

Maybe because, there's nothing else to say.
Maybe because, you took my heart away.
Soulless – and still I wish I could smile again.
You ripped out my tongue and filled your glass with all my sins.

Maybe it's true, that there is no one out there to save me.
Maybe it's true, because I already feel as if I am fading.
But in the end, I might get that one chance to be saved.
I may fight this war because I love you.
But I need only to save yesterday...

Killing Time

Leaves falling, filling the empty space in my heart.
Another season gone, so now I can only wish for one more.
Still I laugh as I remember that you were just a dream.
As all the burning ages fade, I still hear my shallow screams.

They drip further down the spike - then it nails me tight.
As all the pointless faces gaze up at my rotting corpse.
This statement may mean something tomorrow.
But for now it's null and void.

The shouting voices tear my brain apart, one piece at a time.
The locked doors still stand wide open.
"Just another nightmare inside."
All the smoke, of all the years.
That drowns so deep in my salted tears.
Rip me open again to prove your point that I am dead.
Scream at the top of your lungs.
To free this monster from your head.

Waste me again and swim to the bottom of the pool.
Close your eyes if you're afraid, now the nightmare is true.
Face me now or just meet me in Hell.
Kill all the time you wish - *just watch the leaves fill this shell.*

Steaming Tears

It boils out, from both my eyes.
Blistering the skin, weeping as another hour dies.
The acid-tears, they break me down until I have no face.
Still mother sleeps "never to awake..."

Forsaken - but the truth is, "no one cares."
Like a child waiting, from these eyes – steaming tears...
The clock smiles back, feasting upon my fears.
My face melts off, and I know you never cared.

They drip down, and poison the water we drink.
Time fades away, and I'm left with only me.
I would cut myself, yet I've bled all the blood there is to bleed.
These tears boil out – from both my eyes they steam.
I shake and shake you – *still mother sleeps.*

So We Laugh

The lips press against, now logic fades grim.
We hold each other close, as we shadow all our sins.
Time can't hold us forever, "*so we laugh, so we laugh.*"
The earth begins to crumble, an ending at last.

The hammers beat the reason, right from our brains.
A funeral would be pointless, so I decided to stay.
Her tears were a little bitter, behind her sweet smile.
The Devil still grips my heart, as I suffer another mile.

Our sun rips the flesh away, so I weep.
Still I try to forget you, awake in my sleep.
Those lips press against me.
"*Now I'm damned and overwhelmed.*"
So I laugh, so I laugh, another mile into hell.

So, So Many...

There are so many things I would like to say.
Before I wake up and you fade away.

The morning shapes, the meaning of this.
Her nightmares form colder, comforting her wrist.
The ancients hold the reasons, which form us today.
I feel nothing can save us, from all the mistakes we've made.

Biting down harder, breaking the skin.
All that she once feared, now awakes once again.
The emotions of the hollow, now drive her to fate.
We all drink from the broken glass.
Drowning out all our rage.

So many wishes I made, to forget her face.
And so, so many stitches, holding me out of place.

I'm Not Sorry

Like daggers shoved into the back of my head.
Every time I smile, it pains me like a sin.
I've forgotten what it was to be a good child.
Only because you never knew what it was to be an adult.

So the reactions come, I'm not sorry for being right.
Again you fight it, tearing apart the only one who cared.
I can't bring myself to say it's okay.
Not after the disrespect.
"You just threw my heart back in my face."

It's like a million ants biting.
Each and every time I say I love you.
Yet I'll wear it forever on my sleeve.
I am the evil one you hate and fear.
But I'll never say I'm sorry.
Because I know that you don't care.

So Go

Please Jesus, give me some sight through this stagnant haze.
Please lord, hold me close before I fade away.
Dear God, I know it's over now, my heart and soul are dead.
Please forgive me, "but only after I speak *Rage* once again."

Now the time clocks are backwards.
So smile now and sing-sorrow through the day.
Rip the only pure thought from your head
Mix it with the lime, and then throw it away.

Take everything you ever wanted from me and go.
I know now I could never have made you happy.
There is nothing more to say now, to you.
So go somewhere else you must and be joyful in misery.

God... "It's over."

Please Walk Away

Well... I guess I'm back where I started.
There must be a reason, why God plays with me like this.
Maybe I deserve it all or it might just be to get some kicks.
But the one thing I've come to know over time.
Fight all you want but it doesn't make it right.

The eyes watch over, and still can't understand.
The words were spoken and died in my heart once again.
So fear is all I can keep close to me,
I'm so alone, I no longer have enemies.

The concept of failure was never once an option.
Now I turn inside, trying to find where I went wrong.
But all I can see through this darkness, the one thing I know.
If I truly want to save myself, I had better stand up and go.
"Just please, walk away..."

Putting Words in My Mouth

Years of sorrow and fallen tears of insane-cries.
Broken nails – raw, and another germ inside the lime.
It boils through, the painting of that which could never be.
I'm standing now in front of the frame, I smile again and weep.

Those whores were right and so are you...
It was a pretty picture we painted but now they know the truth.
And reality still sets itself aside from me.
I would love to make a great point today.
But you're still putting words in my mouth for me.

Cold as the sun dies out once again.
There's nothing I can do now, to stay warm under this skin.
But again I move onward.
Just to see what tomorrow could bring.
I would love to say something with great significance today.
"But again, you're putting words in my mouth for me."

Sing It Again

Here it goes and once again.
Take my hand and step to the right step of whims.
And sync the correct words to what I feel.
Tell the riddle right and maybe not wake up in hell.

Passion felt beneath, both hopes of now you see...
A heartbeat can mean so much, yet be so pointless in deed.
There is no wrong way, but you have to do it right.
Sing it again and miss no step.
So maybe you can wake up in life.

The Reason For Pain

Years of sadness and tears of madness.
Sanity can't just rule itself aside from me.
So now there's meaning and you see it steaming.
But the longer you wait, the more it dies.

Days of nothings and dreams of somethings.
Now the divine spectator knows when to make his move.
The beast still sleeps and waits to feast.
As another angel strolls off the path.

It's getting old yet still tastes so sweet.
The photo of that child, the sad sideshow-freak.
Torn and consumed and his youth is drained away.
The Devil bides his time, so he can get a taste...

There is nothing more for this sleeper to endure.
This zombie shall never forgive your sins.
And pain has a reason, a purpose and point.
But you'll have to suffer so great before we rejoin.

So take time healing your wounds and scars.
Rejoice in the pain, so maybe you can learn...

94

Stay With It

I'm ready now to take that final plunge into the dark.
I understand now, what it means to tear my own heart apart.
I'm willing to see more than just what my eyes can bear.
Give me one last chance to smile, within this shallow despair.

Those memories still haunt me, so I'm waiting to forget.
The pressure of a mind not rested, it's starting to cause a fit.
But not to worry, because I know the stress could take this life.
I understand now what it meant, so please turn off the lights.

I get the bigger picture now, I understand the tome.
I wasn't ready to leave, yet now I'm all alone.
But I'll stay with it, until the last spot of ink is dry.
I'll be the man I was meant to be, the *Lost Honor* behind your lies.

Keeping it Fresh

Those words, somehow they lost meaning to me.
All the traditions seem false, all the stars shine bleak.
And I go through life, with this smile painted on my face.
With the emotions of a beaten warrior, dead yet still awake.

So I go on further and miss no step, yet I break.
The mirror that reflects me, stained forever with your shames.
But it keeps the tensions firm and holds me close to that spike.
That grave that binds me to the horror, "dark day – bright night."

Laughter ringing onward, of that haze that pushes me deep.
I wish only to end this nightmare, yet I've never found sleep.
That dead-ring keeps me cold, that chill straight to my soul.
The thought of those words are keeping this body aware.
As I lie awake in this hole.

When Tomorrow Dies

The fists slam against, now bones begin to shift.
The logic of a bitter lie, hidden behind your eyes.
A hope now left hopeless, and tears begin to freeze.
Yesterday was only a thought, today was just a dream.

Death holds me as the years break off and fade.
My lover can never help me, because they locked her grave.
This spine holds the reasons, of now it makes no sense.
Maybe I'll understand when I wake up, from this endless night of sin.

Knives push in deeper, as my smiles begin to erase.
I can't save you now, so please "just walk away."
Those minds are just a lost-whim, of now I feel the sting.
When tomorrow dies, I might be able to forget our dream...

Never Was

Under this skin, now it crawls behind my heart.
I know it wants only my death, so I lean in and enjoy the burn.
Those words lost their meaning, now God knows I'm here.
There might have been a lesson, but I know now only fear.

It eats me still and I feel only the bliss.
I know it's breaking me down, that one last kiss.
Noon holds me tighter, to the knowing that I'm dead.
There never really was a reason for me.
There never was, a reason to breathe.

So the demons keep me going, until the nights are gone.
This monster loves my torment, so smoothly it sings along.
Keeping me in tune with my damnation.
There *never* was a reason, so now this soul is left forsaken.

Laughing Loco

Rust blankets over, all the memories of then.
Strolling inside this vision of a past left in the wind.
A reason now forgotten, the thorn that remains inside.
This place seems familiar to me, when I close my eyes.

The voices must know my heartache, because that tone is mine.
The objects of a time left burning, somewhere deep inside.
The ghosts of my past still haunt me, because I enjoy the pain.
As the leaves of then begin to cover me, I just laugh insane.

The minds of *More* - they can't erase me, though they try.
The answer to the weeping, will never heal her cries.
Ages gone and fading, the ghosts of then still remain.
As I try to shadow all my fears, still I find myself.
"Laughing insane."

Tearing a Page

Something of nowhere now taking us further into the pool.
Not an ocean quite yet - your tears drowning this miserable fool.
A bitter turn when you open your eyes to this world of pain.
Just another lie to get us through, one more day in this cage.

Flesh binds us together, yet we couldn't be further apart.
These bones know what you mean, but I no longer care.
A wound can only hurt for so long, now just pointless despair.
It's not an ocean yet, just another puddle of tears.

It bleeds through, as I shove this pen harder inside.
How many words have been said, how many times must I die?
Not all the stars of the night can equal my scars.
Yet I can't seem to just give up, I've come too far...

Empty thoughts still keep me awake at night.
I'm just too numb today, laid under the ice.
"No points to be made - no love at my side."
So just tear this page, and wipe the tears from your eyes.

Scream-Weep

Speak no truth, because you lost the rights.
Seek no freedom, as all hope begins to die.
Tear the thorn out, and place it into my heart.
Nail my tongue to the floor, soon to speak - nothing more.

Beat this body until the flesh is gone.
Tear away any romance, and sell this worthless soul.
Light a candle and search for the right thing to say.
Forget about forgiveness, and desecrate my grave.

Smile as you forever wait for mother.
And weep because you know she'll never arrive.
Rip the skin off the back of my neck.
Shock my spine as I scream, *as I scream*!
"Please God let me rest..."

Dirty Child

No words can describe this filth that covers me.
Gray ashy mold, a world of pain and decay.
Hollow in this soul and alone in myself.
Ruled away, no nerves - insane.
Now reason has gone and no one cares.

Bitter in this pool of mistakes.
Still I hunger, the feast of another human's brain.
And it takes some time to heal the wound.
But the world still fears me, now they locked my tomb.

This ghost remains because I was nothing more.
A child beaten, lying bleeding on the floor.
So get your laughs in and enjoy my mistakes.
As I wait alone in myself again.
Festering in the back of my own brain...

Beat Me - Love Me

Maybe it would be best if I just didn't sleep.
I would call it a nightmare but that's all that's left of me.
I watch it stand there waiting at the foot of my bed.
The smell of lit matches, it freezes the lungs inside my chest.

Thoughts betray me, I'm going down and no one will save me.
The noose tightens and I'm beginning to smile.
Peel away my face, so I can drown in denial.
The notions gone and still I'm broken again.

Yet she throws a smile, for not a reason to be.
She kisses my forehead and shoves the nail through my cheek.
But it passes and I remember the truth about her and me.
So go ahead, beat me - love me.
Because this body has no more blood to bleed.

Cut My Tongue In Two

The walls are spinning, pulsating, driving me further into my fears.
The clock smiles back at me and pulls away another year.
There's nothing to change it, and no one will take it away.
Please God, just get me out of this hollow dream called eternity.

The pills can't shake it, nothing can heal my shattered heart.
All the thoughts of you laughing, still they tear me apart.
As alone in this hell called my own shell.
I hate you but you're all I've ever wanted at my side.

Still you take your blade, and on those words of shame.
You cut my tongue in two and I weep alone, without you.
The walls are breathing, heavy and nothing makes sense now.
My body's failing, breaking under the gravity and I shout!

The mind of a child, left wandering through the endless abyss.
You cut my tongue in two, never again shall I know truth.
Yet all I've ever wanted in return for my strive.
Was just a kiss, "but you left me to die...?"

The Symbol On My Chest

This hopeless push towards something of the past.
What meanings do we need, what reasons are left?
Passion has passed, horror and loss seem to remain.
Justice was never truly *Just* and Sanity was never really *Sane.*

Grace held firm in the middle of what I came to love.
Now hatred would be a reprieve to how empty I've become.
The demons never had the gall and God's angels were never really there.
I've lost everything that had meaning, I lie broken in despair.

Yet through the ashes of this world of disgrace.
I stand once again, shamed, hollow and still no face.
A body seems pointless and these nerves never really worked.
Frayed and bleeding, awake I wander as a lonely corpse.

Pushed against, the hopeless wants of something passed.
The flowers that circle me, they died and now they're ash.
This symbol on my chest, it once meant something truly great.
But now that my grave was forgotten, "*it only stands for a broken faith.*"

The Demon's Blood

What makes this body lift, after Death gives its kiss?
When will this shadow break, and let me drift away?
Will God take pity or do I have no soul?
What makes me love you still, now that I'm dead-alone...?

Will ever this grave you fill, or am I damned to be?
Let this freak move forward, into the last break.
Give some hope to the hopeless, show mercy before I fade.
Love me if you can, give me a chance to correct my mistakes.

The smile still moves me through, the pain of what I am.
A bitter thought of nothing else, a child that can't understand.
For some reason or another, that it was never said to my face.
I lie alone in hell-broken, shallow and disgraced.

But this demonic flesh, it keeps me open.
To the inevitable destruction of all "*Angels* and *Men.*"
This blood of the demons keeps this body going.
But I seem to know, this heart can't meet all the demands.

100

Christ

Wants of the child that waits in his head alone.
Tears of the dreamer that wishes to find his way home.
Another long road that leads to nothing ever-more.
The ashes that hold us together locked behind an open door.

A stone kept in the middle of this frozen chest.
Her smiles pushed me further, down deep in this hole.
That cradle now broken, the infant left to weep and bleed.
A million stars that drip from an open wound.
And it's all your lies I keep behind my teeth.

The monster waking from under my bones.
More wants of the child that waits in his heart alone.
A demon dancing behind one eye and within these dreams.
Christ, get me out of this Hell, and set my soul free...

Too Predictable

A dialect resounded far, echoing throughout the streets and drains.
No gold is left, so give now blood to satisfy what I crave.
Her long white dress, *"indeed she knows the song that I like best."*
She then rides the flame, so no more spirits of our bodies remain.

Torn and it's so great, the part of the chorus that I yearn.
My heart sleeps on the moon, in joy her gravity now blooms.
And sanity seems so distant, because you took it all away.
You can't stop me now, I've anticipated all steps you'd make.

Frail toy, of now all morality has melted with the limes.
There are no more faces to know us, soon we'll both unwind.
No silver bullet can match this grace, *"oh now I get the jest..."*
You were just way too predictable today - so sorry but you failed the test.

False Reflection

What's your name and who the hell am I?
Were we ever lovers or both just biding our time?
Please take this noose off and shove the blade inside.
What meaning do I live for, or have I already died?

A lost state of something that I seem to forget.
You kiss the scar on my heart and pull out the remaining stitch.
So give the razor further into my arm and you weep.
Frozen tears of - you never gave a damn for me...

Mirror behind the being that you called your soul.
Your father couldn't stop me from caring.
Your mother never forgave me for leaving you alone.
So what more could I do, and what else could I have done?

What's your name, and have we met before this day?
Where are we both going, or are we already in our graves?
Please take this false reflection and shatter it against my face.
I wish I could say I love you, but we've already faded away...

Hold Me Through

Age gives it value and time breaks it all away.
Pressure gave us diamonds and a bullet through my brain.
Love was once a riddle, yet now I don't even care.
Passion was a great pastime, now a thought I can not bear.

Fire keeps this body fresh, blistered rotting to the core.
A mind would be a great idea, yet now it's just a stain.
Roses circle this body, a song echoing inside my dreams.
Vanity may seem a little absurd, because I have no face.

The power passes through and God takes it all from me.
I breathe for only the destruction, of the world of my children.
I pray that some day you'll come to understand.
Please take a minute, to hold me though.
"And honor each moment we had."

Grind It

The demon's teeth, left in the dirt and under screams.
A child lost, because he knows that he's all alone.
It takes more than you'd think, and I know it's a lot.
Hold your breath while you dream, *Remembered* before *Forgot*.

A worm below the surface of the dreamer's mind.
A hollow step pulling me down, time after time.
So cut out the heart of the lover and kill me again.
Take my dream and destroy it, grind it down until it's sand.

Soul Sanitarium

A phase that can't shake it - a mark that won't make it.
Lines drawn to show what we've hidden from the start.
Bruised egos and a pile of ash that we can't explain.
Tears over the canvas and blood that can't fill these veins.

Rust pumping and muscles that grip together and cause distrust.
Locked cages and the emotion of now we bear disgust.
Purple neon-slime drips from the pills that never stop the monster's feast.
It's darker in hell - now that it's frozen and I never sleep.

Barred like a beast and beaten against the walls of God's home.
Given to the wolves, "just a sheep" and I can't find my soul...
Of nothing that the worm didn't take at the start of this trip.
Your apathy fuels my rage and my hate fills the pit.

Sick twisted minds that ripen under the sun.
Passion never gives us reason, and then it rips out my eyes and tongue.
Nothing I can do and there's no way for us to escape it.
The sanitarium walls begin to crumble and I can't just shake it.
My soul is dying - I don't think it'll make it...

Chapter 6

Misunderstood

I'm a Minus

Down-broken dreams as now the truth's left awake.
Forsaking the right path, and honor seems as my only mistake.
Too many roads taken and so many more I've yet to seize.
My heart's too far out to regain, it's black, broken and diseased.

Endless needles venturing into the stem of my brain.
"How many more beatings can this body take?"
A kiss from *the Devil* and destruction floods my eyes.
Breaking me down into nothing, defeating all hopes I've tried.

It takes some time now, the lifting of my head today.
There's nothing you can do to stop it, *this soul can't be saved*.
Broken down, so I'm a minus, wishing there was a better way.
Still so many questions inside, too many *Devils* on my grave...

Bitter Gem

Face it clear and take no turn away from grace.
Hands held gently as all our memories begin to fade.
For no other reasons of the bitter soul inside this dream.
I truly wish I could save you my love *yet I can't even save me*.

The logic never helped it but I tried my very best.
I didn't know how to stop it, so I closed my eyes and guessed.
Her mouth left open and I wish I knew what to say.
My thoughts are in splinters and *nothing will ever change*.

So she took it and all my fears ate me alive.
I knew there was a bigger reason, something we can not deny.
The lost hope of a bitter gem holding together my pain.
So she's gone now and I must face the facts.
That some things just never change...

Knuckle Against

Place your fist against this stone.
Try then it fades, so all my thoughts leave me alone.
There's nothing you can say that could change this heart.
Ten million more demons, tearing me apart.

Place your anger unto this stage.
A man behind the broken smiles, memories that begin to fade.
Thoughts that were saved as I wandered out alone.
So push it further, knuckles against bone.

Rage can't beat it, and it's placed against the line.
Satan can't shake it, so he bides his time.
Our fists slam against it, the stone that holds my name.
The knuckles shift behind it, bones cracked and bleeding.
Now screaming in anger and pain...

Nothing + Me

Open screams that can't fill the space in my dreams.
Shallow tears that flood the mind that never cared.
A last moment change and nothing really matters any more.
Mounds of photo albums burning, as I lie naked on the floor.

A spike pushed against and I know it's going to be fine.
A bullet lain on my plate, so I add some spice and give it time.
There's nothing that can wake me, because I've never slept.
There is no one out there, yet still I waste my breath.

This room seems colder and somewhat broken more.
My thoughts are melted now, stuck frozen to that door.
Escape would be great but I know what's on the other side.
These screams help nothing, but it passes good time...

An open scar means nothing, when there's no *body* attached.
These last minute acts are nothing, just great means of naught.
Shallow and alone again, waiting for these memories to rot.
I've given - time and time again I realize the cost of my sins.
The endless price of my screams, so that's all I'm left with.
Just Nothing plus Me...

Of Dying Grace

A million mirrors reflecting each other's reflection.
A standing hope and it all seems vast and unconnected.
The song of the ages plays on and on until the rapture.
A voice not sounding yet I know it's out there.

The fading thought of her gives me a reason to be.
All that I once loved about death has now taken hold of me.
There are no more re-sets to this Game we play.
I wish only a teardrop, upon her dying grace...

Oh too many stars out tonight and I just can't calm.
There is no saving the spirit of the angel, it's been too long.
So many cheers and growing thoughts of truth and peace.
Yet I know of "*the voice not sounding*," over her dying grace.

She Wants the End

Reach in further and take hold of the trash called my heart.
Enjoy the holiday smiles and tear my being apart.
There was once a story about a kiss that should never be.
But there must be an ending, and she takes it all from me.

And these boney hands still hold the answers to our sins.
All that ever held reality together, now breaking-grim.
Yet the moon knows what the child weeps for at night,
Somebody please wake me, some one turn out the lights.

So take the honor and place the trigger against your tongue.
There was once a day that I loved you, yet now it is done.
Over and over so many glasses of blood and wine.
She wants the ending - so I close my eyes...

Closing Stages

A circle drawn and I lie smashed on the floor.
My mouth full of leaves, falling deep to the core.
The eyes in my head have taken a brake.
They roll back to see what's going on, on the other side of me.

There are those things that some people just can't understand.
The ghosts of yesterday, and the monsters under our beds.
We try to give our anger meaning, but I said the truth anyway.
There are some facts of this universe we just can't change.

So read me clear and label me under and full of fear.
The trust of man and demon can no longer be controlled.
I wish I could love you still, but you ate away my soul.
So it's too far out and I'm sorry that you don't understand.
As I enter the closing stages of the positive & negative.
I'll look for you, on the other side of then...

Hush

Hush my child and say not a word.
Let the sound of my voice be all that is heard.
Please let me hold you once more and again.
Hush my child and dream soft upon the winds.

Take my hand and let us venture far-far away.
Weep not my child, please smile again today.
And over the moon you dance with the stars.
I'll sing you a song, which will take you far.

Away with the thoughts of demons from hell.
Let the sound of your heartbeat keep them overwhelmed.
The fear of the sandman will soon pass you by.
Hush my child, please don't cry.

Let the memory of wonder keep you safe at night.
Sing along when you're afraid and just close your eyes.
Hush my child and say not a word.
Just let the sound of your heartbeat, be all that is heard.

Can't Let You...

Time and time again, as I gaze upon your smile.
I reach in deep and spit-up another mile.
Of how far away can my soul leave this body?
Your kiss still breaks me and now the fears are controlling.

Years turning and so many cries have gone unheard.
You grip my spine and rub it gently, wiping away my last nerve.
They knew how hard to push it and now I'm erased today.
It's only your hatred for me - that keeps this soul awake.

I can't let you end this, not after what I've been through.
I can't just sit back and take it, soon I'll catch up with you.
You're trying to destroy all the emotions I've held of Grace.
I can't let you take it and wipe away my faith.

Null the Last Wish

I'm sorry my love and I wish there was more I could say.
It's been so long and all those memories once again fade.
Into the darkness of the pit in the back of my head.
And you place your lips against my heart and null my last wish.

Because the tears could never fill the ocean of my fears.
A last lonely push and all emotions begin festering inside.
I'm sorry that I couldn't be there for you, *but please know I tried.*
I wish there was a better view, as I gaze over into the light.

The papers burn and all the thoughts of then subside.
The hand that held my hand, left and then it died.
But no matter how hard it hits me I remember the pains of then.
And you place your lips against my heart and null the last wish.

For Reasons

For reasons unknown and lain under the stone.
For all the times I tried yet failed.
The years of pain and months of tattered lusts.
Kisses that faded and our bodies become dust.

Words are all we have, that and this strive.
Reality feels weak and again I question why...
For days of mistakes and hours of pointless hate.
Sometimes I don't know why I try.

A moon that falls and our eyes begin to fail.
I told you what's in my heart, only ash and Hell.
For reasons unknown, yet still they are shown.
The meanings behind the name on my grave.

Counterfeit Flesh

I came in with nothing and I'll go out the same.
I know what it takes to be forgiven for all my mistakes.
Yet I ask nothing of you, so please leave me be.
I've done nothing more than wander further into those dreams.

Beyond all the worry and broken-heart screams.
Behind the smile that you wear and under these sheets.
Over and above all that we press against the grain.
I know what's behind your smiles.
As it lies awake in my grave.

I came in with nothing and I'll leave just the same.
So take note of this encounter and make no mistake.
So hide all you want, behind that husk you call a being.
But I understand your smiles now.
"You were nothing more than a counterfeit dream."

Painted Over

Alone in this room, my jaw gripped to the bone.
Teardrops rolling down my cheek, freezing my hollow soul.
Abandoned and I'm waiting, for something to end the tone.
As I lie broken on the floor, hoping for hope.

My fingers can't make the cut, so they cut away.
All that ever mattered, now it lingers over and never fades.
As it wakes under and can't bear to see the light.
It's painted over, the nerves that control my eyes.

I'm weeping louder, but nothing sounds anymore.
I'd bite my tongue to watch it bleed.
Yet it's already gnawed to the core.
So I hope, hopelessly alone - painted over, on the floor.

Freak of the Norm

Porcelain faces gazing over into my head.
Shallow pools of hatred steaming within my dread.
Taken over and over again I know it's my time.
They hold the shape that completes me, the riddle behind the rhyme.

Shoved further within this shell known as *Rage*.
An empty carcass cast out and left astray.
They beat it senseless and enjoy all the dreamer's cries.
An outcast somehow woven into the story, hidden just under the line.

There was a time, a point when all the answers came together.
A period when all the pieces fell right into place.
But now I'm shunned, and labeled as a heretic in disbelief.
As all the porcelain faces gaze over and into my head.
I stand, as a righteous freak of the norm.
Haunting your dreams to the very end...

The Bullet That Made a God

Time holds together the bonds of man and legend.
Honor grips us tight and holds us to the lesson.
A song ringing through and a voice that keeps us safe.
As we lay our heads to rest and tomorrow becomes today.

Lifted higher and held in our hearts with grace.
A smile never forgotten - those words that must never fade.
A lecture given and a path that holds brothers together.
We try to keep it flowing, for maybe just another day.

Grim as it became so cold and another brother fell away.
Time seems so cruel, as now his legend is etched in stone.
As lost as we may feel at times, we are never truly alone.
It breaks us truly, as devils tried to destroy a great friend.

So now we weep with pride, over the riddle of the bullet that made a *God.*
As those songs play on, keeping us true to the lessons he gave.
When honor grips us tight holding firm that smile on his face.
We remember our brother with love, and will cherish each other everyday.

Conformity

The bells ring on and nothing moves me anymore.
Spoken words repeating, a numbed elegant-chorus.
For naught a meaning, as we are driven onward to grace.
Holding hands as we plummet, a mile below our graves.

Divine thoughts given and the Devil still laughs.
The angels are weeping today, as we're led to our deaths?
With open heart and a pocket that reaches the ground.
We must speak their words in tune, or to hell our souls are bound.

Keep me locked up and under the ashes of the damned.
Their party seems so touching yet I still don't understand.
For what reason should we follow the masses into the flames?
God doesn't hide in your mouths, so speak not his words to me.

I've given my dues, said what I needed to say.
I need not to follow your conformity, to understand my own faith...

Psycho-Phases

The mirror speaks an unending echo that gives an ominous sense.
The shadow that contains me can no longer hold together my skin.
I'm coming apart at the seams and I don't want to break.
As I watch the words drip off my tongue - I know it's too late.

Far out and beyond any hope of regaining my shattered heart.
The truth of now it's left frozen beneath my many scars.
You can't control the monster, he knows what you think.
Try yet you'll fail and it feasts upon your dreams.

I'm sinking, further into the pool of disgrace.
Time is only time and this body begins to feel the quake.
For no pill can calm it, the truth that brings the scream.
The mirror laughs as I breakdown and it shatters as you weep.

Callosity

Gray leaves falling over, and the street begins to turn.
Echoes of ages passed and my lips still feel the burn.
Dust bleeds from the open sores at the bottom of my feet.
Blood fills my mouth as you smile, and inside I begin to scream!
Hands hold over and take me towards what I fear.
I ask if anyone understands, "*but I don't think they care.*"
As it pushes against and another life is taken away.
The road rubs me harder yet the leaves hide my shame.
I'm waking louder and so much has gone unsaid.
Still it echoes on through the haze that lingers in my head.
While ashes fill my eyes and the streets seem to have no end.
The ages rub harder against me, until I have no skin...

The Blades Come Nigh

Dancing shadows and faces that remind me of her.
She has no name today, because all my memories have burned.
I'm not waiting for forgiveness, nor have I forgotten.
I want only to dream, beyond all the horrors of this nonsense.
It's getting closer and I think it's going to take its toll.
The blades come nigh, cutting away at my soul.
There's no saving this being that you label as just a shell.
The blades are coming closer, as I awake in hell.

This Monster Knows

You're running and running, deeper into chaos.
Steaming and screaming, for someone to save us.
Yet nowhere is nothing, that equals your disgrace.
You shower and cower, bleeding just concrete.

Some time, alone in a rhyme - letting the master hold the key.
So sick, and some trip - weeping over the cradle.

It's waiting and hearing, you're breathing quite softly.
Running-decaying, and hoping for reasons.
Yet nothing is no one, that needs a new outcome.
I know that you're crying, for justice in chaos.

Some time, a shallow crime - damning this bitter soul.
So sick, a pointless trip - *and yes*, this monster knows.

Valiant Velocities

Speed to the ground as I lie awake unfound.
Bearing the rhythm of now it's getting good.
Taking no resource beyond any recourse.
And I smile because I know what it's gonna do.

The lights flash and reality passed.
Please forgive me for not kissing you goodbye.
Take note my sweet and add spice to your dreams.
Because I'm coming home and coming soon.

So valiant of an atrocity, that screams with such velocities.
I know what you want to say, "And I do too..."
So pity not what lies dead under the stars.
Give respect to the game we play, and make no remark.

Unseen as it runs through and breaks away the flesh.
Such a cynical reframe that holds not what she said.
The screams of the speed felt with the angels atrocities.
I take all pride to be had, with these valiant velocities.

In Two Hands

A day that passed by and left no better strain.
Such a twist of no one cared, and I guess it's the very same.
When logic grips the stem and I begin to know no truce.
All the visions in my eyes seem bleak and so are you.

It was only your sweet words, now forming a bitter taste.
In my mouth I hold the answer that you can never take.
And it's making me sway, I'm feeling the sting.
In my heart I know you hate me, and in my ears I hear the ring.

I'm melting away and draining down the sink.
The picture I hold of our forgotten love now begins to freeze.
You're not letting go, and I can't take this anymore.
I hold your ashes in my two hands, and I weep as the wind takes its course.

Respected & Dead

Ink still binds me, giving me shape and contrast.
Charcoal gives me details and keeps together my past.
I'm running out, I've done all there is to do.
Pain gives me a motive and there was a time when you did too.

I'm not sleeping, not until the spike has been driven through.
"I can't keep my eyes open."
So I rip them out and hand them to you.
They have no structure to what they call their lives.
Still I lie awake in question, and I don't know why...

You visit me on occasion and I am grateful for that.
Yet I need no more pity, so I turn my back.
She loves me still, even though she spits on my grave.
I hold honor as the respected and dead.
"Awake I endlessly question, why I've never found sleep..."

Odium

For what reason need I give.
Of a dying thought left bitter, rotting in the pit of your fears.
That voice that seems to call out, when no one's there.

Did you never care, or was it just I?
Did Satan show you justice, did God give you the time...?
There is no brighter outlook, only what has come to be.
You can't hide yourself behind the dirt, "*because I can still see....*"

Loathe me my lover and let us reign in hell.
Kiss me and let us not take another moment of this dance.
We're reaching further and I'm going to take what is mine.
For what better reason need I give?

"And why for you, should I waste my time...?"

A Melody of Massacre

Unawake today, and all at once my memories begin to fade.
Humming soft as the choking-grip takes its hold.
A million years of fire, burning away at my rotting soul.
So now it's passed and we're so – so cold.

A lifeless meaning and a heart left dead.
Words of a mother that gave us birth, and then she turned her head.
Blades begin to warm me, a smile on my face.
Songs that play down the hallways, leading us to disgrace.

A bitter poison and a torn page that lingers on.
A melody that runs on in my head, as all the air leaves your lungs.
Dying in horror, as tears and spit flow onto the ground.
Unawake today, and mercy cannot be found.

Fading and leaving, because it's so – so cold.
This armor is still bleeding, as I hum this soothing tune.
Ages of fire and burning-ice in my rotting soul.
Yet I still laugh as I destroy you.
And at last the choking-grip finally takes its hold.

Tsunami

Lifting us higher and the ground falls away.
Holding us closer before you turn the page.
A soulless want, because you were my lover.
Now an empty void of undying discomfort.

Under – so many miles as it pulls us away.
Rushing against the bottom, now the sky turns gray.
My head in the clouds and my thoughts begin to scream.
You slowly tear me apart, because I was just a dream.

The walls reach the heaves as I lie awake in hell.
The hopes of being forgiven now begin to fail.
Emotion ripping us frantic as now it's time.
Done – and I fade away, when she closes both her eyes...

Nonsense

This is the end of lying pains.
Bitter souls that dig inside and try to remain.
This is the last of my shallow wants.
The blood on my face feels warm as it dries in the sun.

You were the last, of my great loves.
Now the snow gets deeper as it fills both our lungs
You are the answer to the nonsense and aches.
As I lie alone in myself trying to justify my mistakes.

This is the end of losing sight.
There are no more reasons left when you turn off the lights.
You are the nonsense that infests my brain.
The bitter memories that dig inside and try to remain.

Love was the answer to the jest.
But time took its toll and it was for the best.
So this is the end of all things to be.
The insanity that builds inside as I smile and scream...

Keep Running Away

Constructing a new view of concealing rage.
No points of consideration beyond these thoughts of pain.
Burning-nails glowing as they are pushed under my flesh.
Her smile still breaks me down, soon nothing to be left.

Winter grows and the leaves rot inside my heart.
An age of decaying loves, now grim and torn apart.
A child then, but now I don't know what I've become.
Destruction beneath this skin, dripping hatred off my tongue.

Reasons dim, as I'm judged for being - *a man of my word*.
Demons held far within, gripping my spine as I slowly burn.
I can't keep hiding, buried under the filth and ash.
Yet I still keep running away, trying to destroy my past...

Backwards-Dream

Backwards-dreams unsatisfied.
Her voice so sweet but then she died.
Lost hopes of running behind the stage.
Pleasure found with assorted pains.

Dreams now boil when you're under the drink.
Love so worthless while this heart still sinks.
Miles taken while the Knight didn't look.
Your soul forsaken for every life you took.

Endless dreams beneath frozen stars.
Soundless screams as you rub these scars.
A voice not sounding but I know it's there.
I'd ask for help but you never cared.

Backwards-dreams and undying hate.
Love left bitter as it rots with my pains.
Endless hours of pointless cares.
So I question myself, because no one's here...

Nimbus

Beyond any hope when you welcome the voice.
Numbed legs giving in and I begin to feel the void.
God reached out his hand yet I couldn't see.
This nightmare goes on nonstop, and it's all because of me.

Their drug lifted me higher, but then I began to fall.
With my eyes glued shut, I see nothing at all.
This torment builds up until there's nothing else.
All God's angels weep, as I fall deeper into hell.

These hands know the reason of why the oceans burn.
My tongue senses no taste so I slowly learn.
As this body knows anger and nothing really helps.
The voice took me under, now I drown in rusted nails.

Please give me guidance and bring me back to light.
Take me out of this sulfur and open my broken eyes.
I want to rise into the clouds and feel the awesome of peace.
As nimbus lifts me up to the stars, I begin to understand grace.

Chapter 7

The Turning Leaf

Shifting Forward

Ten fingers holding together my shattered face.
Another day of waiting, for a new twist of fate.
Time runs its course and now we're nothing but faded ash.
Must my mind still push further, until reality has passed?

Smoke fills my heart again, and it's nothing you can change.
My hands remain damaged and worn, forever left stained.
When romance calls and all we feared becomes a grim fact.
I still move myself forward and never look back.

Anger rules it and no one can comfort my soul.
Ten fingers keeping me together as I shiver so cold.
Time takes its toll again and nothing can change that fact.
For some reason I'm still shifting forward and never looking back...

Smooth Remedy

The eyes in my head are turning black with misery.
Words keep this body moving yet nothing can cure me.
Shallow when night comes and now the facts are here.
Sorry is such a pointless notion, so I swallow my lasting fears.

Anger seems great today, yet I'm only beating myself.
Torment of another sunshine, and I accept the hand that I am dealt.
No one can save me because I never did exist in this life.
Try yet you can't cure me, "only waste my time."

Love left devastated and still you're laughing at the tome.
The girl who is "*weeping for her dead lover,*" and still she's all alone.
Candles burn in a circle and all of the laughter fades away.
So I will drink your smooth remedy, "*yet I just can't be saved.*"

The Drowning Meek

Modest smiles across the room and she doesn't really care.
Winter becomes a prison in this soul, so sorrow seems unfair.
The match burning and darkness fills my aching mind.
Six feet over my head, under water I slowly bide my time.

Gripped firm in my hands and she knows what I'm going to say.
Sorry - and my thoughts splinter, festering cold inside my brain.
Judgment calling and I know it should have been me.
So I lie down under water, dreaming both shallow and meek.

Fire taking and nothing makes her want me more.
A stone that holds me, shamed and disgraced to the core.
A modest smile and she laughs the way she always did.
Winter becomes a personal hell I endure time and time again.

Shaking - the last note and the candle wax covers all that remains.
She took my last words, and now I have nothing more to say.
Judgment calling, and I'm so sorry but it should have been me.
So I rest my head under water, *Forever & Always.*
"The drowning meek."

Spider On My Tongue

When nothing meant everything and you knew my name.
Joyful laughs of brothers and yesterday stayed the same.
There were those remarks that dug deep into my soul.
Now a blanket of ash covering my every last thought that I hold.

I can't speak it, for the words lose themselves with me.
I can't take it, now the pain creates the steam.
The spider on my tongue, it's eating away at my hopes.
Its web it tightens and covers my fragile soul.

It takes no pity and I'm thinking this is the end.
As I fall to the concrete and it smashes against my head.
A spider on my tongue, spinning its webs over all my words.
I can't take this any longer, so I close my mouth.
And accept the venomous burn...

I'll See You...

Give me time on this and let me shake your hand.
Speak your words again and kiss them upon my lips.
Leave it all at that and let us breathe once more today.
Guide us to the river, so slowly we drift away.

Grip me firm to that and make me know you're here.
Burn my eyes with the fire and laugh at my frozen tears.
Wave your hand again, side to side it swings.
Give me time to say it right, just before you leave.

Not to mean nothing of no one cared from the start.
Speak what little we have to say and then we'll both part.
Beyond and over all that we said meant the world to us.
So I'll see you when I see you and goodbye until then...

Behind this Face

These scars keep me up at night, so I smile at the flames.
Anger kept me open to rage yet it's all the very same.
This bitter taste feels soothing now, because it is my time.
All the pictures of my memories burn, so I watch it all subside.

The moments flutter and nothing keeps me centered any more.
So much blood given, over these meaningless wars.
I'm so sorry my friend that it ended so cold that day.
I am truly sorry but still the sorrow hides behind this face.

Shame takes its toll again but I guess that's all I've had.
Darkness bleeds deeper into my heart, filling me with dread.
No more hopes to seek, so I lie blind and weeping on the floor.
The scars behind this face keep me up at night.
So I wait, "*behind an open door.*"

Dying Alone

I guess you were right and I should just admit to the fact.
There's nothing more to say now, so I'll just rest.
I've done so much and it was somehow all for you.
But the story is over now and I must accept the truth.

It's colder than I thought it would be, when it'd come down to this.
So I lie my head down and try to remember our first kiss.
But nothing can help it today and somehow I'm feeling weak.
So you were right after all, and I just need to get some sleep.

My eyes begin to burn and I understand what it's for.
This room seems colder than it has ever felt before.
So I try to remember all the joys of our yesterdays.
But I'm dying alone and cold.
And yet somehow it all feels the same.

Gently

Gently the bones begin to scrape across the teeth.
All the hours spent on her smiles begin to fester inside of me.
She wants me to love her, no matter what she said that day.
I kiss her lips once more and spit out the acid taste.
Of a day not taken when we all know what it means.
Over so much of a deception that I just can't let be...

So soft of a tickle she feels across her breast and face.
I can't bear the thought of injustice "*but it can wait.*"
It goes gently across the blade and I love the sound.
All thoughts of this moment feel disconnected and unbound.
It all takes its course and I so enjoy this feel of bliss.
Gently I smile once more and give her a last kiss.

Great of a moment taken and I keep it to myself.
All thoughts of regaining the pains of now I know it's hell.
She said she wants me to love her, no matter what she did that day.
So gently the bones begin to scrape across the teeth.
Of now it's over and I keep all the pleasure for me.
So softly it goes as I kiss her lips once again today.
And gently I smile, as I spit out the acid taste.

128

Stirring Voice

So many months of tying to put up with these screams.
Tears come to my eyes and I wish I wasn't me.
But this must be the price I have to pay for all my sins.
So many nights of trying to sleep, as I feel it stirring within.

My body aches so much with the worries of yesterday.
In my hands I feel the burn and nothing takes it away.
So I begin to fall and I know I'm going to hit very soon.
I feel it stirring inside, the voice that reminds me of you.

So cold that day and now I feel the chill once again.
Please give me my last-rights so I can disregard all my sins.
Tears come to my eyes as I walk down that hall today.
The stirring voice in my head reminds me of you.
And I just wish it would fade away...

Taking Its Toll

I was only a child and still they locked me away.
I was once your lover but still you slapped my face.
Salt bled from my wounds and now I'm empty inside.
All the ages of the world begin vanishing, far- far inside.

Whip me with a wire and let me know the shock.
Cut my eyes in the middle and drink my blood on the rocks.
Push me harder against the ground and now I feel it steam.
Reach your hand into my chest and rip out my hollow dream.

I'm only a sad child wishing there was a happy end to this.
I was nothing more than your lover yet you spat our last kiss.
Away and now it's taking its toll on my frail and broken soul.
I'm too empty to care for you today, so here I wait.
All alone – all alone.

Raving

It breaks me open and now it's spilling out.
Am I crazy to think you loved me? *"Truly without a doubt..."*
This moment shoves its way in, into the back of my mind.
This war is breaking me down, so please turn off the lights.

So another age dies and the leaves begin to turn again.
Was I not the one who was there, to warm you under my skin?
The void has said all, what it needed to say.
So am I crazy to think you ever loved me?
"Without a doubt in my brain."

Unaided – Un-held

Forever it drips deeper into my wishes of being saved.
So they place their tongues over my stitches.
Now I only hope for some guidance beyond this haze.
I'm falling deeper into the core of what you call Hell.
I wish I had feelings for her but now I'm only a hollow shell.

Mother tries to wake me but I only hear the scream.
Their shadows choke me softly, so I just let it be.
I wish there was an answer but I've yet to find a single breath.
No one seems to help me, so I just enjoy all the stress.
I feel it shaking, so please give me one last guess...

Forever it drips deeper beyond the whiskey smiles.
I still feel abandoned, so I suffer another mile.
They won't let me rest today, for I am breaking at each touch.
Unaided as they lick my stitches away.
Un-held as my reality slowly fades into dust.

In the House

My hands feel the sharp pain, as time rips out my eyes.
The ages of a fallen memory, now it haunts my demented mind.
The loves of a day I held her, now she's only ash.
The wall spells out the motive but I just can't let it rest.
In my heart I know I'm leaving behind all that was truly me.
In the last moment of my life I would just like another drink.
So many ages of this broken man, the unending story of a turning leaf.
In the house I'll leave the answers, to all the questions that you seek.

Foolish Heart

So many miles away and years before the screams.
Inside of the man not rested and beyond his failing dreams.
There was a day that became as dark as the night.
Inside his aching soul, behind his burning eyes.

She gave that look and there was nothing he could say.
He wants only to feel some hope beyond the tormenting shames.
So many tears flowing and songs of love that gently fade.
His heart won't let him rest, so he lies awake.

The stone comforts the horror of what is yet to be.
Tomorrow became a notion that can never calm the screams.
Such a foolish heart and she takes it away in spite.
So many miles away and still I feel the pain.
Behind these burning eyes.

When You Said Forever

Give me that look again and let me feel your heartbeat.
Say that you love me and tell me we'll never part ways.
Fill my dreams with your laughter then kindly smile at me.
Tell me that I was your great love, as I slowly begin to sink.

Your words meant the world to me, once upon a time.
Now I'm frozen in space, cold as I dissect my own mind.
Your kiss gave me life that day yet now I feel the chill.
Give me that look once more, before I swallow another pill.

Light gave us warmth, on that day that became years.
Your lips gave me hope, now just hollow tears.
Tell me that it means something more than what I know.
Please say what I want to hear before you let me go.

When the time came and I knew I was right.
Before we took that walk far beyond the night.
When you said forever, did you think it would end like this?
So... Now it's over and forever that is it.

All That's Left

As I lean my head back, I watch the smoke flow over my eyes.
Insanity seems so tantalizing but I just don't have the time.
There's nothing to do now, so what am I fighting for?
Can anybody hear me? Oh never – never more...

The passion of torment begins to lose its luster.
So I leave the rusted nail in and watch it tear at my mind.
I'm slowly losing grip of the rage that keeps me alive.
So I hammer out my brain just to bide some time.

So that's all that's left of me, I am only a demon today.
Give me a better purpose beyond my shallow shames.
As I lean my head back I watch the clock begin to laugh.
Insanity seems so pointless today but it's all that I have left.

Locked Inside

It's freezing my eyes closed yet I can't look away.
The ground soaks up my blood, forever stained.
Shattering any hopes, so now they take control.
What am I doing here, "I just want to go home."

The bullet takes its stroll further into my lungs.
The gravity of the moon holds me down.
So tell me, when will this be done?

It's freezing my eyes shut yet I can't look away.
All the emotions died tonight and slowly faded away.
So what am I doing here, locked inside someone else's head?
Please let me out, before the both of us are dead...

Join Me

Take a seat and rest your thoughts, be calm.
Please hear what I'm saying, it won't take long.
Have a drink and relax your troubled soul.
Put your feet up, as you join me through the cold.

We're going to drift softly through dawn.
Take my hand and please hold on.
Hear what I'm saying and take note, okay...
Take in a deep breath and count, 1 – 2 – 3.

Join me into the darkest pit of your fears.
Awake in the shadows of these damned aching tears.
We're going to stop now beyond all the scorching hate.
Go ahead and open your eyes, before it's too late...
"Join me."

The Rose She Held

She stood there weeping in the rain.
Her tears steaming in the cold as they rolled down her face.
She stayed there waiting for an answer to a question unasked.
She stood there weeping, with a rose in her hand.

Could she be comforted in the darkness of her shames?
For what reason unknown, as she waited out in the rain.
Her fist gripped tight as then the thorns began to tear inside.
While she waited for an answer, unknown of why...

Her lips gave a quiver as she held the sorrow in.
Her soul became heavy with the burdens of her sins.
She stood there for hours obsessing over the question unasked.
She stood there weeping, with a rose in her hand.

A notion taken as she waited there in the rain.
Within the tears from her eyes she carried all the blame.
Her heart began to quiver as her soul became cold that day.
As she waited with a rose in her hand, standing over my grave.

8X8

Tearing behind the back of these eyes, only to see what's next.
Ripping the minutes from the clock as this mind tries to rest.
All I truly want today, is a meaning for all my pains.
A sacrifice received for motives of torment in which I never did believe.

Now the struggle takes its grasp on my remaining nerves.
Numb as I wish someone cared before this heart was burned.
Does this name hold meaning or am I just another blank sheet?
Please tear me apart now and let this dreamer sleep.

War has taken its toll and this mind has done its share.
Time still wishes to haunt me so am I never to repair.
The shaking heartbeats are destroying, all that I've strived for.
Still I hear you laughing behind the open door.

Mercy never helped but it was a great start to this song.
Now these bones are growing weaker as my hatred moves on.
Time flows constant, and I wish you were here with me now.
"Would you calm me down my love or just cast me out...?"

Tearing away at the back of my mind, just to find release.
As I burn within your nightmares and again you laugh at me.
It's been a long trip and I guess it took its toll on my soul.
Does this name hold any meaning or am I just a sad dream?
For now I'll take a step forward and let my heart find some sleep.

What Remains

Judgment pulls further as I'm pressed against the stone.
Logic seems cluttered so I stand once again alone.
The purpose of the falling – I wonder as I wish to hit.
To remain under the ashes, forever wrapped behind the stitch.
Her waking speech, holding me against my broken nerves.
This snow won't seem to melt so I wait, hoping to learn.
The nonsense of the demons keeps me aware of my rage.
So I speak nothing more because we never had much to say.
What remains, other than this shell of what could never be?
Who holds my heart today? Because I know it's not me.
Judgment pulls me deeper into the darkest pit of my fears.
What remains of us now, besides these lonely tears...?

Mother's Ruin

She whispers it far into the back of my fears.
She tries to hold me close and wipe clean the frozen tears.
I've fallen against myself and now my heart wonders why.
She tries to comfort me and soothe all my pointless cries.

So night-fall has taken away any hope of ever seeing light.
She tries to wake me while I'm screaming but I don't know why.
It's colder here, now that my body has taken all damage to be.
She whispers it far into the back, trying to save my failing dream.

Smoke begins to drown it, far under the thoughts of peace.
Tranquility seems so distant because I can no longer see.
She wishes only to cure what ever it is that drives me into myself.
But she can't save me now, so I begin to watch this body fail.

It's drowning all hopes of ever finding Hope.
Nothing can awake it now, this frail and miserable ghost.
I've fallen against myself and hate me for whom I am.
So I smile as she drowns me further, under the golden sands.

Divided

This surface seems tattered, broken into scattered shards.
This flesh is cut into thousands of sections.
Rough as you push your fingers against the scars.

Rubbed against the grain and it feels so bizarre.
This checkered outline of my body begins to feel the burn.
Divided as I lie with my head thrust into a wall of stone.
My surface seems so disconnected so once again I wait alone.

Then you place your fingers between two fractions of my skin.
You spread them apart to see what may lie hidden within.
Divided and my checkered surface spills out all that I've held.
It feels so strange as I'm torn open and you gaze into my hell...

Choking

The words elude me when I'm put on the spot.
Her eyes so stunning and my heart is left in shock.
I feel my emotions swaying as I try to not stare back at her smile.
But there's not much I can do, just breathe in for a while.

She takes it all in and what could I truly say?
I can't find the words now, so how long should I wait?
Her laughter lifts me higher and I feel that spark once again.
She looks into my eyes and I feel my sorrows melt within.

The words elude me when I'm put on the spot.
Her smile haunts me and my heart's left in shock.
I feel my emotions swaying as I stare so dazed at her hair in the wind.
But as I try to say what I truly feel, I find myself choking again.

Vanishing Act

I place my hands over my eyes to hide from the light.
I sit alone in darkness hoping someone might understand why.
I try to erase all the visions I hold of a love that could never be.
I push my fingers into my eyes hoping to be set free.

The actions consume me as rage gives such a great rush.
But the pills still bleed from my heart, as it festers in a pool of distrust.
This room feels colder, as I lie broken on the floor waiting to give up.
There's nothing you can say, now that I've run out of luck.

The whiskey melody dances its way into my spine once again.
As I bury myself under the charcoal and wait within a pathetic sin.
The stars try to find me and I want her to know my face, never-more.
Again I push my fingers into my eyes hoping to vanish – out of sight.

The darkness of my shallow wants brings only pain and fear.
So I intoxicate myself with all my sad and lonely tears.
Watch closely or you might miss this act of erasing my being.
So I begin to vanish before your very eyes, hoping only to be set free.

A Glass of Pity

What comes to mind when you speak my name?
Was there a great purpose of my being or was I just a mistake?
Tell me what you think of me now – now that my body has left.
Could there be a great ending or am I damned like all the rest?

What vision comes to your heart when you hear my words?
Was I more than a great moment in your life or just another bore?
Tell me there's something that keeps me tied to your soul.
Could you truly care for me or am I still waiting here alone?

What gives me purpose now, other than the spike?
Was passion just another dream or was I even truly alive?
Tell me you have one shot left to keep me warm through this daze.
Could there be a happy end or will I just be erased?

Hearing Your Words

Her face stands out when the smoke softly subsides.
In this blue night of lying awake and biding my time.
Her smile moves me still, years after the fact.
It's quiet these days, yet I still hear her voice when my eyes begin to rest.

Can laughter determine the outcome to a night of grief?
Will the liquor truly calm my heart or only amount to more disbelief.
In the conclusion of heartache, I know *Pain* remains as a concrete truth.
I'm hearing your words again, yet they're pointless without you...

Her face stands out in the crowd when I realize I'm all alone.
Her voice sounds so sweet today, hidden far beneath the tome.
It's quiet now yet I can still hear your words ringing when I try to rest.
Can laughter truly determine an outcome, or is it just a waste of breath?

A Shallow Step

What is it in her tears, that makes me wish I were dead?
I promised I would never hurt you *my love*, but in the end I did.
Still I'm trying to make sense, of the muffled screams that night.
What were you trying to tell me, before we turned off the lights?

There're no answers, to most of the questions I ask.
Still I move onward, taking another shallow step.
Her whisper tickles my ear still to this very day and I open my eyes.
What was it in her smile, which seems to be forever etched in my mind?

The clouds fall short and torment beats numb against my spine.
So I take another shallow step, hoping only to buy me some time.
Still her laughter eats at me, while the smoke pours from my lungs.
What was it in her eyes, that makes me laugh as I load the gun?

Waking Dawn

The long hours of the night – but I guess it's become the day.
The chill as I light the cigarette, and exhale in pain.
Destination seems so futile, now that I understand *the greater cause.*
The rain stabs me ruthless, as I wander further into the *lost.*

Shame holds together the makings of this bitter sound of rage.
As I stroll deeper into the morning, I wonder if I'll ever truly awake.
The long hours of the night – but it's not quiet today.
I understand now, what it is from which I've been running away.

Another step and my bones scrape against the road.
The rain freezing me brutal, digging straight to my soul.
Destination seems so futile, now that I stand here at the waking dawn.
So I move forward into the night, because I know it won't be long.

Guilty

What ran through her head when she walked in that day?
The smell of burning pencils and _Hell & Heaven_ cut into my face.
Did she understand what was going through my heart at that time?
Loss and regret building beneath the years of pain and neglect.

Did the other feel sorry after she tried to take her life?
Was I at fault for being heartless, am I guilty for laughing in spite?
Did she ever care about tomorrow or only that present night?
Was I truly the one to blame, for not caring and laughing in her face?

What ran through her head when she walked in that day?
And she followed me into the backroom, where she realized _"I had no face..."_
The smell of whiskey bleeding from the mirror in the hall.
Am I guilty for being a ghost, should I be blamed for having survived?

Did God intend for this to happen or is this all my fault?
Was I really that cruel back then, with a heart made of salt?
The demons try to comfort but the fact is that I am damned today.
Am I truly guilty of loving you and will I be judged for walking away?

Chapter 8

Casualty

Mindless

A casualty casually laying his head against a stone.
Resting his eyes, waiting for his ride home.
The sunset holds a sheet of sadness over his tired eyes.
As the moon begins to lift and yesterday slowly subsides.

In his mind he walks back to that one place that he holds in his heart.
With all the visions of his love, as she dances with the scattered stars.
He rests his tired head waiting and hoping he'll be home soon.
As he dreams of laughing, under the glory of the moon.

A casualty casually laying his head against a stone.
Resting his eyes, waiting for his ride home.
It's been a long trip and his heart trembles as daybreak draws near.
But he just rests for now, as his love - she sheds another tear...

As the Crow Flies

The smiles of decades passed, now faded memories begin to relapse.
The old love whispers a teardrop into the ocean of my tired heart.
As the blade of last winter slowly begins tearing me apart.
Her eyelash disintegrates as *Mother Earth* sings our souls to bed once again.
Not all monsters of this world feel pity over those constant futile sins.

Your child weeps asking for sight in this concealed reality of pain.
Your body shaking as you lie inebriated, stirring under the rain.
No amount of rousing can shift you off that track of "*Bitter Dismay.*"
As dawn subsides you gradually understand the meaning of yesterday.
You can push only so far before you start stumbling over your mistakes.

As the crow flies overhead we notice that our bodies were only dreams.
The constant struggle to get what has meaning before it all slips away.
The endless pushes and fights only to realize that pain will never change.
You've said what you needed to say and done what you needed to do.
We've been where we've needed to be, yet as the crow flies overhead we notice.
"That our entire lives were nothing more than a fleeting dream..."

With Liberty

Take the spikes of shallow hate and nail me to our burning flag of hope.
Justify your ignorant whims as liberty drowns beneath all your sins.
Lift the child known as the answer to the prayers that we've sought.
Burn him now and laugh as independence is torn down and lost.

Fight my brother - now, give haste and let the blood pour.
Swift now, and watch as the sky turns red and the flames of hell slowly burn.
Justice raped and taken so show no mercy to the thieves.
Be ready to die with honor, never stop until all of our children are truly free.

So now it's taken beyond and justice fades as another soldier falls.
That last candle has melted, so now in darkness freedom is lost.
Fight the struggle and push back when they throw you against the ropes.
So with both liberty and justice they will nail us to our burning flag of hope.

And it Falls

And it falls to the side.
As all my loves begin to die.
So irony slaps my face.
As I'm left alone out of place.
Nothing takes me further than this.
Ripping out the very last stitch.
No more wishes left to help me now.
So they all laugh as I'm cast out.

Blood is flowing from my eyes, hopefully soon I'll understand why.
Time is rotting away any hope, of ever reaching that last page.
My name was taken, so tell me who I am.
And it falls deeper, beneath the graveyard sands.

Hopeless hoping for my last rights.
So hurry up please and turn off the lights.
The irony slaps my mouth once again.
As I slowly drown in all my sins.
The thought of leaving has taken its hold.
So tell me why do I feel so cold?
As the blood is flowing from my eyes.
And it falls as I begin to die.

144

Against the Darkness.

Take those last words and lead yourself beyond any whim of hate.
Bite your lip harder until your mouth fills with blood and rage.
Follow the zombie to the edge of the pit that is your bitter fate.
Slam your head against the darkness and scream because you're too late.

The sand still falls into the open shadow in the back of your head.
Time pushes you further and now you wish you weren't at the end.
Loveless lips press at the back of your dream that holds no grain.
And you wish to fall against the darkness and forever there you will stay.

Take a number now and remain deep inside your aching head.
Tear your skin off and bathe in a pool of broken glass and sand.
Light the fire and watch as all your loves melt hopeless yet alive.
Throw yourself against the darkness and alone you bide your time.

Tears Are Shed

It rolls down her cheek, now her soul is growing weak.
The failed chance of regaining love after burning this page.
All that she once said, now it's gone and shifted within.
The last try, to reach the top and see the light...

The rooms are failing and the paint reflects no joy.
The smell of smoke lingers, as the itching notion begins to annoy.
Her lips are heavy because she had so – so much to say.
Now alone, in this bitter conclusion of misconstrued rage.

Her pride has perished as has her sense of hope.
Now on her last words she slowly begins to choke.
The solitary emotions, she can't bear as her thoughts become weak.
Now her tears are shed, as she lies alone under the sheets.

For the Child's Love

Tense it falls the reason of - when you didn't look before.
Now the mirror holds the answers of ever never and so much more.
The lips press a lie against the grain and now it's far too late.
This child wishes only to be held – only to be held...

The clock dances its way to the back of their heads.
Time laughs as now it will be left forever unsaid.
The fight because, she's the reason as to why this body holds no soul.
This child wishes only to stay warm under the snow.

Tense it falls for reasons of - it's too late to save it now.
The endless battle to get, what ever it is that we can get out.
Her lips press a lie further until it shall remain as a thorn.
So you killed for the child's love - for *Ever Never* and so much more.

Before & After

Laughter leaving behind only a scar in the memory of this.
Days that held so much meaning but now I slowly begin to forget.
The time you touched me and I knew it was love so true.
Yet now as we meet again I realize I never really knew you.

Those days when you laid your head on my shoulder and smiled.
Now I try to open my eyes and see down the spiral.
Can anyone remember the times when I bled for only your grace?
Now I wait hopeless in front of the mirror, grinning with no face.

The shattered flesh still contains the meaning of what I felt.
As now I regain the motives and venture back into hell.
Before and After the times we said we'd hold each other, always and a day.
It makes sense to me now - now that I remember your hate.

The Emotion Called Pain

There it all goes, as the flame races its way into my heart.
All the poison drips down and bleeds from my shallow scars.
The reason lost, of now you can't say it wasn't you – *"it wasn't you."*
And I can feel that you're smiling, as you hammer another nail behind a tooth.

She called it passion, yet I never felt pleasure beyond the pain.
She said she wanted more, more of the ashes from my grave.
The salt rained down and filled the heart of this beast.
Cold and unaware, as now it roams as you try to sleep.

Please get your kicks now, because I don't know when this is all over.
So there it goes, digging deeper beneath my scars.
All the time, she said she wanted a reason beyond the fact of dismay.
So I took her there, one step further than the emotion called pain.

Those Pictures Burns

Those pictures burn in the middle of the room.
Faded echoes linger on, haunting this zombie's tomb.
The film blisters and dissolves, erasing all the hopes for which we've strived.
I wish only to hold you once more before we turn off the lights.

Those pictures burn, destroying all the memories of our youths.
Now as it melts away, I can only dream of forgetting you.
The love we shared and now in tears, I hope it all just fades away.
Our smiles burn now, soon only ash and bitter decay.

It's pointless now, for your face has been permanently ripped away.
Those pictures burn and the fumes are slowly engulfing my brain.
"All the smiles and times we held each other so close with love."
They're burnt and gone, engulfed in flame - dissolved and flushed.

Beneath My Tattered Skin

The taste of a clove, the bitter sweet smell of flesh as it fries.
The rolling of a small pill that brings on anger as all the emotions spill.
It's falling deep to the so-very-far-away, so in grief we begin to scream.
Timeless timing the moment of when the words shall bring themselves forth.
Hidden within, the secret lost forever in the endless void.

The taste of a clove, the great feel of our lungs caving in on themselves.
Now the whiskey tears it open, deep we swim into the waking hell.
Lost with no help, yet we try to scream for a line to the peak.
Yet it falls short and we remain in darkness, both ashamed and meek.
It's burning these scars as you and I remain hidden behind these bars.

The thought of a clove, the awesome feel of this tattered sink.
"Rough" the last point, of the bitter corpse left alone – covered in sin.
Now your emotions run black, as you begin to fester beyond the act.
Such a lack, and no one can hear our cries for help, below the waves.
So we hide beneath our tattered skin and there we shall remain.

Innocence Decays

That smile haunts all the steps I take into the dark.
Her laughter pierces me deep behind my heart.
The black-coal remains as I wish to exist.
Innocence decays, due to all of her sins.

The fear in these eyes shows only regret.
She loves my torment and gives me no rest.
My last chance has come to rise above the dread.
That smile still haunts me as I venture into my own head.

Nothing takes it further than the smile she gave.
No one could ever forgive me for all the mistakes I have made.
The moldy decay remains as I wish only to exist.
Innocence decays as she laughs once again...

Within & Out

I want to go further now, beyond any hope.
And watch as it decays inside, then sinks beneath the smoke.
So what makes me real, other than the pain?
Who was I then, within and out of this prison we made?

The answer falls bitter and there's nothing more to grasp.
I take that next step and tumble over as I laugh.
The starlight shines still, yet only when we blink.
Left within a shell and outside of your dying beliefs.

I want to go further than any of the hopes I have already tried.
And to watch our memories freeze, stuck under the line.
So what makes us real, other than the actions we forget?
Who will I be, "*Within & Out*" of this world so sick?

Another Scream of Rage

Cancer holds me harder, the blackness of my lasting scream.
Destruction of a universe that never meant a thing to me.
God spoke the riddle to a monster within the womb.
Did he expect an answer given, far beyond the tomb?

Folded flesh over the razor then it separates along the seam.
Acid shoved inside, breaking down this body with dread.
Lift the tongue higher and watch as the snake begins to sing.
Kiss her on the mouth and now you accept the dream.

Flushed heartbreak and the last thoughts erased.
Destruction of a universe beyond another scream of rage.
The Devil took the motives and left us with only spite.
As now you understand the meanings of the ghosts in the night.

Decades Fall

Sliding down the spiral of smoke as it leaves my lungs.
Decades fall beneath the lake so now it's soon to be done.
A shaky voice that wishes to speak to her one last time.
To reach out and feel that grace is still frozen behind the rhyme.

A blockade now shifting yet that's the life you chose for me.
So can I take another step upon that road of leaves?
Beaten, so bruised and hoping I'll awake before dawn.
Doom has taken its hold, so I begin to sing my song.

The decades fall, as another rant has been driven out.
The tears from my heart and the needles from my mouth.
It's all been etched deep and set for you to follow in line.
But I don't think you can follow, the riddle that flows behind the rhyme.

As She Wishes

Ash tastes sweeter, when it's scraped off the bone.
The virus of the norm, infesting your fragile soul.
The cries of a child, abandoned in the cold darkness of yesterday.
Take my hand if you wish, yet we can never be saved...

Fly above the wonder, of what lies beyond the stars.
Lift your eyes to the answer, resting behind these scars.
Hope for the hopeless, if you wish to waste your time.
Taste the sugar within the middle, of the demon's spine.

Shake the ice of the graveyard, and drink of the wine.
Fall dizzy with no care, and laugh as we unwind.
The ashes taste sweeter, when it's scraped off the bone.
And as she wishes, we shall wait forever in darkness – alone.

The Demon Cries

Should I have to reach into the burning coals to justify my sins?
Would you help me once more before the sleeper wakes again?
She told me to wait here and take no step towards the edge.
It's been centuries now, so can I finally rest my head?

The demon weeps because my face has faded with time.
The monster's gone-starved as it crawled into this mind.
The piles of ancient bodies have fallen into the pit.
So try to hold on tighter because I think this is it...

Should I have to reach my hands into the flames to justify your sins?
Would it matter if I took that last step over into the bottomless pit?
She told me to wait here – it's been a century, "now I'm just faded ash."
So the demon cries because it knows our ending has passed...

Given Low

The vines have crept far enough into my heart of coal.
The angels want some more – to feast upon my soul.
The light dims but only a bit, so we can still see the fool.
I feel tied down deeper, sunken below the pool.

Fire rains harder, it beats down against my thoughts.
The infestation of my spirit, I fear that I am lost.
Given low, the meaning as to why I have no remorse.
The wretched actions of your society, damning this innocent ghost.

Have I offended our king, today with my screams?
The howling as you drive the nails further inside.
It's given low, the meaning as to why I feel burnt within.
So God dims the light a bit – then watches as the angels feast upon my sins.

Beyond Any Doubt

As she stared up at me, I could see the fear in her eyes.
As she said she would always love me I felt my heart begin to die.
So awesome now, the last chance I had to save my soul.
Beyond any doubt, that she was truly that cold.

Reason shifted forward and now the rim has been shocked.
In the prelude of the forgotten story embraced and now it's lost.
As she gazed up into my eyes I could see the shame she held in her heart.
Beyond any doubt, that we took it one step too far.

Was I the only bastard willing to admit the crime?
I fought and bled over her honor and watched the weaker ones die.
So was I insane? Mad to think there was a chance that she truly loved me.
I know beyond any doubt, that I have justified all the screams...

One More Hope Dies

Twenty filters can't save us from dancing within the flames.
I'll be responsible but I can't promise tomorrow will be the same.
So this is my brain, locked in front for all to see my strives.
As I lie down at the gates, wondering if I was ever truly alive.

The pulse grips harder the meanings we hide behind the line.
The rope's a little too tight, yet still I step over and with a smile.
So I wave to you and you wave at me and it was such a nice salutation.
The clouds formed the last letter so now we welcome new intentions.

Twenty filters can't save us from our grim yet inevitable fates.
I'll be responsible but only after the day I awake.
So this is our brains, locked in the projector showing our futile strives.
So I'll wait at the gates and laugh as one more hope dies.

Take Me With You

Take me with you when the credits begin to roll.
Wake me if you can, so maybe I'll not feel so alone.
Open my eyes again to the sight of what was never meant to be.
Kiss my lips with a smile, burning so sour yet sweet.

Take me with you when the moon falls from the sky.
Shake me hard, until I finally open my tired eyes.
Drag me deeper behind the stage and slap my face.
Hold me close, right before you cast me away.

The hoping now, that there was some meaning to all the screams.
I truly wish you to remain in my sad and hollow dreams.
So open my eyes to the sight, before it passes and leaves a blank sheet.
Please take me with you, when you finally go to sleep.

When the Atoms Weep

Whatever happened, to the world beyond the stars?
Why only when I feel Death, do I confide in these shallow scars?
What truly happened to the smile at the end of the page?
Where will we all go, when the atoms begin to weep?

The memories all decay of the smile you gave, on that day that ended in freezing rain.
Her bones became dust, moldy ash and a more bitter shame.
The bullet whispers, as it dances its way into the back of my head.
So alone that day, the dawn that was best left unsaid.

So what ever happened, to the dreams that hang over the moon?
Why only when I feel Death, does my hatred begin to bloom?
So what truly happened to the angel that I once so very much adored?
And where will we all go, when the atoms begin to weep..?

Night Blisters Behind

Can you taste the paste that's stuck to the roof of my mouth?
The voice that's locked inside, it wants to get out!
I CAN'T SAVE US TODAY, IT'S TOO LATE FOR PEACE!
As night blisters behind, another demon is denied release.

The falling needles, why are they sinking into my lungs?
The failing demon, it smiles with a laugh as it loads the gun!
I CAN'T TAKE THIS ANY MORE, IT'S TOO LATE FOR PEACE!
And as night blisters behind, I forget my own face.

Yet it's only a phase, at least that's what they're telling me.
I know you're disgraced, so get the hell away from me!
I WON'T SAVE YOU, IT'S TOO LATE FOR HOPE!
As night blisters behind my eyes, it combines with all the smoke.

As You Dance With Grace

As you dance with grace, I can see that smile upon your face.
Clear is the meanings, that lost all meaning, before it even began.
Lost unaware, below all that's clear, buried beneath the golden-sand.
Driving it all through, between me and you, so maybe we'll understand.

Taken below the note, right before the choke, that takes it all away.
Is it an irony to you, that I stumbled upon the truth, *years before the end?*
Was I ever truly a noble man, straight from head, down to my bloody roots?
Lost and unconsumed, the meanings behind, all that I have said.

As you dance with grace, I can see the carelessness upon your face.
So damn me if I ever attempt to take that away from you.
Lost beyond the clear, drowning in my tears, as I forget what she said.
Driving it all through, between me and you, and our hoping that maybe someday.
"We might both understand..."

154

Logic Begins to Reverse

The staircase seems darker now, somehow I lost my way.
I reached out for a mirror only to see, I still have no face.
What ever to say, when it comes down to faith?
Forgive me father for having taken your name in vain.

What leaves me aware, other than the smell of her hair?
Tormenting me into a demonic fit of rage.
It is darker now, I don't really know how.
But I must escape this demented maze.

The logics reverse, so was that truly my curse.
I never meant to hurt her the way that I did.
So give me the tools and I'll show you a fool.
Just as soon as I regain my face...

So Now We Plummet

Bite the bullet, so now we plummet deep into the sea of hate.
Step over the chalked-outline, and dance the riddle beneath the rhyme.
Take me with you when our hearts decay and truly we'll never be the same.

I tried to save us a moment, but now it's come to this.
So did I leave an impression, when we shared our very first kiss?
Beyond any thought of warmth, now hidden behind a stitch.

Bite the bullet, so now we plummet further than we'd care to go.
Step over the chalked-outline, and hold your heart very close.
So take me with you, when both our hearts have decayed.
So from that point forward, we'll never truly be the same.

Drowning in My Eyes

Swimming through her hair, lost – I cannot see.
Failing thoughts as I begin to drown and scream.
We're running from the torment, praying as I scream!

To know it's gone further than the emotion called pain.
Shame as she laughed because I have no face.
What was I thinking and did I ever have a chance?
Save me God! Please satisfy my ego with another pointless rant.

Where did it go, the salt beneath the bone.
Now torn sweet and I feast upon the meat.
Take me with you if we're going to end this stress.
It's great to watch you laugh, your hatred I did love best.

Swimming through her hair, blind – I cannot see.
Failing gasps for air, as now my body becomes weak.
We're drowning in my eyes, dying as we scream!

Because I

The morning after, was that the thought I held?
The burning shower, blistering rusted nails.
Was there a meaning or was I only a sad ghost?
I can't remember anymore, maybe that's what I chose?

The simple thought, of regaining some pride today.
Why is it that all I'm ever left with is inevitable shame?
The morning after, was that the pill echoing inside?
Can you hear it now, the abandoned child's cries...?

It was left bleeding cold and alone on the floor from the womb.
Now a drop of acid lies hidden beneath each and every tooth.
Because I cared about hurting you, "is that why I failed?"
Because I tried to help you, "is that why I'm in hell?"
Because I truly don't know if I'll even survive.
Because I loved you, that is why today I die...

Embrace the Silence

The hollow sound of a trigger as it's cocked and pushed in place.
Now my mouth is dry, no longer bearing a single taste.
Dim are the candles that circle me on the floor.
Covered in red, the blood stains on the door.

A whisper that tries to make its way through the years.
Yet nothing rises above the sound, of these bleeding tears.
I can't shake the feeling, that I'm already burning in hell.
I wanted only to save us, yet I was too overwhelmed.

The hollow sound of the trigger being pulled back slowly.
Pressed against this outline, where I should have a human face.
So I embrace the silence, ready and willing to take the next step.
So as I pull the trigger, I let out my last breath...

"Embrace the silence."

Our Hearts Subside

Welcome to the nameless push that just can't take us there.
Throw away our last kiss, dead deep in despair.
Our hearts are burning inside, the pain has taken control.
Look me in the eyes, and tell me I have no soul.

When anger grows, it becomes a tool of rage.
When the stones have been thrown, that's when I fade.
The bitter side of this story is, that it truly has no end.
Because it's already over and you've thrown me away again...

Let's try to smile as our hearts subside and decay.
A burning lump of coal masquerading as a heart of faith.
So welcome to the nameless drive into the dead part of me.
Go ahead and do it, set this demon free.

Our worries are fading now, because we're already dead.
Let's try to say it mattered, right to the very end.
So cut this chest open and rape away my failed dreams.
Let us allow our hearts to subside, so that our souls can be set free.

Chapter 9

The Truth.

Migraine

She gave a smile that drove the nail in a little deeper.
I feel the laughter, separating me from all that was there.
She holds me while I'm shaking.
Her hand over my mouth, taking my air.

They push it in a little further.
And my thoughts run deeper inside to hide again.
The actions of that bitter recourse.
Holding you against your own sins.
Biting down *a little harder.*
Just to see what might bleed out of this skin.

She gave a smile that pushes hard against the strain.
I know you're laughing at this outline that should be a *human* face.
The memories of "her" hold me while I'm shaking.
Echoes ringing within my tormented brain...

"Worst To Worst."

What gives you the right to say who will stay and who will go?
What the hell were you thinking, and who the hell would know?
There could be a reason as to why you hate yourself so.
But I don't think we'd want to hear it, so just pack up and go...

If worst comes to worst, I think we can make it through the storm.
If we try really hard, I think we can survive without remorse.
The waking ghosts are feeling a little fed up with your games.
No one wants to fight your war, so just go the hell away!

What makes us rise, after our feet were taken and sold?
What makes you think, we're happy being this cold?
There could be a reason as to why you hate yourself so.
But I truly don't think any of us would care to know...

If worst comes to worst, I think we can make it through.
If we think really hard, *we were* happier without you.
So go ahead and say what you will.
Yet worst to worst – "we were already in hell."

Evaporating Emotion

It seeped so far, the words beyond these aching scars.
It felt so hard, the bone that tore-out and rubbed against the stone.
So please tell me why - do I still feel so alone.
The evaporating emotion taking me down, erasing my soul.

I'm nothing now, "and never was."
It's over now, filled only with dust.
You're angry today, because I survived.
You've got nothing to say, because I'm alive...

It seeped so far, the words that filled this empty *heart*.
It felt so hard, to take it out and tear it apart!
So hurry now and tell me why – am I so - so alone.
As all my emotions evaporate, erasing my unholy soul.

Shaky Laughter

The thrill of knowing that no one's here to save me now.
Still I find myself hoping that I'll one-day get out.
Her shaky laughter is proving once again my point.
Yet I wish only to smile, as I venture into the void.

It's so heavy now, the price has risen twice today.
Logic tells us to stop, yet still we move on the same.
It's much darker now, now that you've gone away.
Still her shaky laughter drives this dreamer insane.

The option of failure, "what was it that you said?"
I wish I could love you, but I'm already dead.
Still I find myself hoping, that I'll some-day get out.
Yet I can't forget her laughter, *so shaky and full of doubt...*

Lending a Hand

Lending a hand was never really my choice.
Yet still I find myself fighting between our words.
For freedom never truly existed in this life of pain.
As I look back I can see only demons, stabbing my brain.

The symbol on this chest, it's divided and spread out for all the rest.
This name - that once held me in check.
It faded away - with her very last breath.
Yet still I find myself finding-out, that these voices will *never rest.*

So lending a hand was never truly my choice
Yet I find it so funny, that you thought it was a better course.
So freedom was never truly free in this life of pain.
Still I lend my hand to you, *in the hopes that one of us will be saved.*

Not My Choice

Her lips pushed against my lips on that day of losing grip.
Her eyes told me to dive in, let out my breath and quit.
Her hands grabbed me hard and held me close to her heart.
But I'm too empty now, alone behind these scars.

Her lips pressed against my lips on that day of giving up.
Her eyes told me to let go, and sink beneath the mud.
Her hands grabbed me tight as if she'd never let go.
But it's cold today, and I'm still alone.

Her lips pressed against mine on that day of trying to quit.
Her eyes told me to leave it, and walk away from those sins.
Her hands grabbed me cold, as ice if I didn't know.
It was not my choice but still I'm alone.

Between Our Words

The smiles faded away, because you were never real.
It's still so many miles away, these wounds will never heal.
I'm falling into a pit, which seems to have no end.
But again I hit rock-bottom, beneath the sea - *wishing I could swim.*

What makes you better than me, other than your lies?
Who said you know me? "You'd better get this right."
What have we to stand for, other than our pride?!
What better reason do you have than that? "*It's a good day to die.*"

Between our words, is that where society stands today?
Between our faiths, was reality God's only mistake?
I'm falling into a pit, which seems to have no end.
Headfirst I hit *and laugh,* between our words of sin.

Fighting For Freedom

The smoke tells a story of a time when peace was genuine and true.
Now I can't kill myself without being reminded of you...
The smoke tells a riddle that seems to have no end.
So watch real close as I rip off my own skin.

Anger gave us nothing that we didn't have from the start.
So one more bullet on the back of your tongue "*just burning out.*"
What have we here, laid dead on the floor of this scope?
So try all you want, but we've ran out of hope.

The smoke tells a story of time of peace and love.
Now I can't even kill myself without messing it up.
You can fight all you want for freedom that is truly *just.*
But the truth is - this is a war that just can't be won.

164

A Better Lie

It gets me through this darker time.
You get me through on this bitter lie.
So show me mercy please before we try.
Quick! Do it now, before we all die.

It gets me through this pitch black hell.
Your better lie and you'll never tell.
So show me remorse before you let me go.
Quick! Do it now! Let's eat this angel's soul.

It gets me through this darkest hour.
Now time has passed and all is past.
So show me honor when you end this page.
Go ahead and tell your better lie but still you won't be saved.

The Truth...

Go ahead, give it a try, try anything you need.
Because the truth is, there is no truth.
Only the lie you choose to believe.

That's all there really is, so in the end *"were you ever truly free?"*

Go ahead, just let it go, and breathe in all the air that you need to breathe.
Because nothing really matters.
Only the sightless sights that none can see.

That's all there ever was, so in the end *"who were you to me?"*

Just let it go, and go ahead and begin to scream.
Because no matter how much you give.
There is always more blood for you to bleed.

That's all there could ever be, *"so Unjust and so Unfree."*

So go ahead, give it a try, try anything you need.
Because the truth is, there is no truth.
Only the lie you choose to believe.

Stranger

Hello again, so where are we standing now today?
This room feels a little colder but I know it's the very same.
These words seem over used yet I haven't reached my fill.
We can try all we want yet this pain will never heal.

Good morning stranger, it's been awhile wouldn't you say?
Still you stand there smiling, as if nothing at all has changed.
So what's new with you, other than the obvious facts?
You can say what you want, but I know you're holding back.

It's great to see you again, *"it's been too long I say."*
This pain has grown a bit and it won't seem to go away.
Maybe next time we meet, I'll tell you something neat.
It was great to see you again stranger, but I've got to go to sleep.

Freeze-Dry

Darkness fills the broken chalice known as this heart.
The winter chill sets in once again only to tear me apart.
Her smile continues to haunt me, so damn my un-waking dreams.
Her kiss it still scars me, *"so please my love just let me die in peace."*

Her laughter breaks me again and I wish her lips against mine.
I can't shake the memory, of when she loved me to the end of time.
Hatred wishes only to drive me away from all the aches of this.
So frozen within, laid beneath a stone of ice - still cherishing that perfect kiss.

Darkness gives me my only chance of ever knowing peace.
The snow brings on a chill that digs its way into my dreams.
Her smile forever haunts me, and I just wish her lips against mine.
Her kiss still kills me, as forever those memories lie frozen in time.

Those Eyes That Betray

Dim... The night that she pushed me against the door.
She kissed my neck and led me into the backroom for more.
She pushed me down on the couch and let the music play.
As she put her legs around me, then I noticed those eyes that betray.

She wanted me to let go and to just enjoy the ride.
I only wanted one thing that night, just only a smile.
She told me to exhale and feel the bliss and grace.
I let her have her way, as I stared into those eyes that betray.

Her sweat tasted so sweet on my tongue that night.
I'll never forget the moment when she turned off the lights.
She said to hold on, so I put my hands around her waist.
Connection of an Angel and Demon, as I fell in love.
With those eyes that betray...

Particulars

The light crept into the hall through a crack in the door.
Muffled voices could be heard weeping but nothing more.
The old thought of regaining a small chance for hope.
It's over now, and these lungs begin to fill with snow.

Am I back where I started? I'm beginning to think it is so.
Was there a reason I was forgotten, I guess I'll never know.
So why is it that I've been abandoned once again?
There's nothing I can do to change it, *"so I step over and enjoy the winds."*

What was it, the fact that kept me moving all this time?
Where were you, hidden just behind the shallow rhyme?
We all wanted something for something but we gained nothing in the end.
You always walked away from your child and there you shall stay.

The light crept into the hall through a crack in the door.
I waited all alone, hoping I'll gain just a little more.
It's over now, all the particulars of our yesterday.
So once again I am forsaken, just waiting to fade away.

Agony

Waking in the middle of the night.
Breathing out the fire as it spreads onto the floor.
Destruction of an angel's wings.
Torn into pieces as she began to scream!

Waking in the middle of a nightmare.
Knowing that she just can't be saved.
All I've ever truly wanted.
Was to just stand up and walk away.

Agony can't describe it.
The pain that fills my broken heart.
If you're brave, then you can try it.
And for you I'll weep, as it tears you apart...

The Child That Survived

Mother smiles as she sips from her drink once again.
Laughing in denial, as she takes someone's *hand in sin*.
Mother's happy, as she enjoys the Devil's drink.
She laughs the night away, as this child lies alone and weeps.

Nothing can save it, the one that was left screaming alone.
But mother's happy, as she steps further away from home.
No one can hear it, the child that's left in darkness and fright.
Does mother even care, for the child that survived?

Mother smiles because someone handed her another drink.
She laughs behind her smile taking someone's hand for "*sleep.*"
So mother's happy, as she plays the Devil's game all night.
But mother never truly cared for me, the child that survived.

Dancing Bones

Truly no one knows what it's like inside this skull.
Would anyone care to understand why this body feels so cold?
It's different now, yet nothing has really changed.
These words seem a little stronger yet this soul has become weak.

She took my hand that day and guided me to the lake.
It was there where we knew our destinies would collide.
She took my hand and said it would be okay.
She said... *"Don't be afraid my love, you're only going to die."*

Truly no one knows the truth behind this story of war.
Would anyone care to know how it ends, before we shut the door?
It's different now, the voice that speaks from this soul.
As these bones dance through the night, trying to stay warm in this cold.

Black As These Lungs

It looks red, the steaming lump of flesh I spit out today.
What am I going to do, what would my love say?
It looks a little darker now, the light has gone gray.
I can't breathe any longer, so soon I'll just fade away.

It feels cold yet as if my lungs were on fire.
What will happen, when all my dreams begin to retire?
It tastes like blood, the liquid that's pouring from my mouth.
My body aches, God please get me out!

It looks like no one's here to save me now.
I'm all alone, so it would be pointless to shout!
It feels as if a million demons were eating me from the inside - out.
The blood has become as black as these lungs.
Now I know there is no way out.

Alone On the Floor

Where am I and why am I lying on the floor?
Who am I and is there a reason why I feel no remorse?
The ghosts have all said their goodbyes and left.
So tell me why - am I out of breath...

Alone in this room that seems so strange.
My body trembles and my heart begins to shake.
The riddle feels familiar for far more reasons than I know.
Please someone tell me why – am I all alone?

Where are we and why am I broken on the floor?
Who am I and why is this pain getting worse?
The ghosts have all wept and said goodnight.
So as I lie alone on the floor, I slowly close my eyes.

Add Some Lime...

Go ahead and take your time.
If you wish it, then please just add some lime...
Hold your questions until this is all over.
The lights are out, now we can hear the rolling thunder.

Salt bleeds from the open wound in my heart.
What makes you any different, what soothes your aching scars?
The burn still keeps it moving, the thought that I can't bear.
Go ahead if you wish it, and add some lime to this eternal despair.

It helps the taste, as it burns and stabs its way to the core.
What have you to say, for something never more...?
The river of salt still flows deep inside my chest.
If you don't like the taste, then just add some lime and hold your breath.

Morbid Memory

The field was warm that day, the sun hanging in the sky.
She had a smile that day, it filled this heart with light.
We took a long walk, into a hope of something more.
She gave me a kiss, now it's only a scar that my heart can't afford.

The darkness creeps in, shadowing and feeding all our sins.
Hatred begins to bloom, feasting on destruction and bringing on doom.
The last word spoken and she told me it was all okay.
Now hell has taken over, and dust has filled my grave.

The field was warm that day yet now it's frozen in time.
All the morbid memories, still haunting me till the day I die.
She took my hand and we walked far into the hope of a better drive.
Now damnation has taken its toll and we weep as we all go blind.

Drowning In Tears

Insanity – was that the only thing keeping me in tune with Rage?
There was once that mask that I held over this face.
It's gone now, maybe to a much better place.
But for some reason or another, I know this was your mistake.

The only lesson learned lead lasting legions of labeled lunacy.
Hardheaded heretics harping hatred heading for humility.
Open outrageous opportune outstanding obligatorily.
Fear forsaken for far further forthcoming frantic fortunate fortuities.

The dying grace, the only lasting memory beyond those days.
Tearing inside to find what was and could never be.
There was that mask, now only a thought of unrivaled humility.
As now it gets deeper and I sink, drowning in tears.
While mother laughs and this demon screams.

Follow the Flame

Follow now and watch as the sky becomes gray.
Look closer now before it just fades away.
Take a moment please and enjoy the bliss of rage.
Let's take one more step and laugh as it's all the very same.

So light the flame and watch closer to see the smile.
Look into the eyes of the snake and let us dance down the spiral.
Kiss the stone because we are nothing more.
Follow the flame that leads one step, behind the open door...

The Blood That Rains

It's steaming now, the wound in the middle of my chest.
It's over now, well I guess in the end - I gave it my best.
She's weeping for me, because I know she's sad.
It's raining again, soaking the ground where I stand.

The missing piece, she found it once but said not a thing.
My aching soul, today it's nothing more than a permanent stain.
I'm dying again, over this tormenting sense of deja vu.
It's raining still, flooding this shell – reminding me of you.

It's colder now, so steam still bleeds from the open wound.
It's over now, because love after all was truly pointless without you.
She's weeping again, but maybe it's not for me.
Oh the blood that rains - it keeps me grounded to the bottom of the sea.

Waking Asleep

I found it waiting, the last moment when we both laughed.
I think I was a great chapter in her life, yet still she threw me back.
"There was a time when nothing could stop me from loving you..."
I fear now that it's all over, now dreaming seems so pointless too.

This river of sand breaks on through all that stands in its way.
All the cuts on my chest, still can't match the scars on my faith.
She knows what I'm saying even if no one else could understand.
Please tell me goodbye, before I drown beneath the golden sand.

I found it waiting, the child that once reflected all my strives.
I hope she can remember, but now they're turning off the lights.
"There was a time when nothing could change the fact of how I felt for you."
Now I'm waking asleep, and dreaming seems so pointless without you.

Random Shots

Go ahead and do what ever it is you think is right.
Cut me open, maybe just to see - what's inside.
Take a shot at me if it'll make you feel like a man.
Do whatever you must do, before I rise again.

I'm taking my time with all these notions of feeling so bleak.
What ever truly mattered, now it's gone and we're too weak.
Timeless times I told the truth, only to fail in the end.
Take a shot at me now, because you won't get this chance again.

Shake me hard, to knock loose what ever it is that's inside.
Lose all emotion you held for me because now you're out of time.
Cut me open so maybe you can just get a laugh.
Do whatever it is you must do, before I rise again.

Replica

Worst of sentiments, when it came down to the matter.
Lost all of what I strived for, then I drown in all the laughter.
Years have been taken, our youths are all now passed.
Lost in a graveyard, beneath a thousand years of ash.

Life was a diversion, to get us through the day.
Death was a convergence, so now we have our way...
Respect was an obligation, but now you've crossed the line.
Honor will be found, so please just give it some time.

Worst was the outcome, when you addressed the matter at hand.
I lost all that I could cling to, so now you begin to laugh.
Years have been taken, all our hopes are now dead.
Lost in a graveyard, reflecting a replica of their pasts.

Clone My Heart

Please my love smile for me, don't be sad today.
Please understand, and laugh all your worries away.
It hurts "I know," but you must be strong - be brave.
I know you'll miss me, and I'll miss you the very same.

Don't be sad when the music stops and all the smiles fade.
Don't be lonely my love, because I'm at your side all day.
I know it hurts you, but you must be strong "okay?"
Just close your eyes when you get scared and wish all the pain away.

It's darker now, and still the clouds begin to rain.
It's over now, so please just smile today.
Just remember me as who I was, remember all of what I say.
If you remember me...
Then truly I live on in your heart, forever and just a little more.

Faceless Smiles

Burning candles light the room where she rests.
As this failing heart still echoes from deep within this chest.
The hours were taken and all the laughter was a sham.
Nothing is the same anymore - nor will it ever be again.

Endless it grows deeper, the thorn now piercing my spine.
Eyeless sights now being seen for what they truly are.
No one can hear you now, all your screams have fallen short.
Still faceless I smile, laughing with no remorse...

Me vs. Me

Now all these things in my life.
They just seem to be another knife to pull out of my heart.
Once more I'm placing that blade back between myself and *Me*.
Fighting the mirror only to realize, the one simple fact I never wanted to see.
In the end of all things to be, I was truly all along battling "*just Me.*"

She said I should smile as the nails are pushed further into my eyes.
So how many more miles must I walk before I can just rest my mind?
It's been so long, I no longer know if you were real or just a dream.
I don't want this pain any longer, so what must I do to be set free?

Time spoke the riddle to my heart when I was only a child.
Now mother has left me alone, so I swim in the fire.
I was once a leader, now I'm a heartless clown without a face.
I loved an angel once, so I was cast to hell for all my mistakes.

Who was I then, the yesterday that haunts my every step?
Tell me how will this end? Well I believe I did love you the most.
But the mirror still wishes to take me down once again.
I've known all along, I am the demon that feasts upon your sins.

Now all these things in my life just seem to be another knife.
The blade that stands between myself and Me.
I've fought this war for far too long to just turn my back and let it be.
So in the end, after all the battles are over it will come to be.
The true trial of this war - *Me vs. Me.*

Chapter 10

No Time

Tilted

Life is pain – death is pain, sorry that I was insane.
"Was I not the man that you wanted me to be?"
Sorry love – sorry mom, but I can't keep holding on.
Not any more, just let me be free...

Truth was lost – at a cost, that I couldn't pay.
I loved an angel once – but they took it away.
Now in shame – alone I break – just waiting to scream!
This demon wakes – my hatred aches – get ready to bleed!

So where do you go when it comes down to this?
First against your head, and then across the wrists.
I pull your knife from my back and watch the wound bleed.
Damn I was a fool, to think you ever cared for me...

Illusions

I can still see her smile behind all the layers of smoke.
A million things I had to say but again I began to choke.
We shared a smile and laughed over our drinks.
It's so great to be next to you my love but now I begin to sink.

Whatever truly mattered, it's now gone-done and dead.
Whatever it was you said, I think it was for the best.
So what am I to say, when no one's there to hear?
What am I to do, as I drown alone in all my fears?

I can still see her smile, years after the fact.
My body feels likes it's failing, so here's the knife from my back.
We enjoyed the time we shared, even if it was only for a second.
Sometimes I miss the illusions, of the angel that created this demon.

She Wanted it Forever

Indifference delivered dividing all that we know.
Dancing in a perfect circle, letting the demons eat our souls.
Salt on a beach where she said that we should meet.
"Now that I think of it, I was never the one who cared..."

Love left in the middle of a burning field of wheat.
So we eat all the ashes hoping maybe we'll learn to believe.
She told me I was the only one that she ever truly loved.
Now I begin to laugh - lying six feet beneath the mud.

Sinister it begins to break its way inside.
All the things I loved about her, now it begins to die.
She wanted it forever, the fact of her and me.
I wanted only tranquility and to maybe find release.

Drawing Behind

Disconnect me from this race you call humanity.
Violent you begin to tear inside, taking all that's left of me.
What will it take before you understand this eternal war?
Now I take another step and dive headfirst into the endless void.

Shelter is all that this heart truly hopes for today.
If I try real hard, maybe someday this soul will be saved.
It's funny to think that there's nothing more to say.
Yet this mouth keeps moving, to keep my aching mind awake.

Disconnect me from this race you call humanity.
Slap me in the face and teach me about humility.
What will it take, before you understand what's drawing behind?
Now I think I'm ready, so please just close your eyes...

The Lesson Lost

He fell tumbling down and no one was there to catch.
He was stunned is what he was, because they all began to laugh.
Nothing could change it any more *"no heroes here today."*
But he stood once more with pride, as he ripped off his own face.

They laughed at his wounds and rubbed them with salt and lime.
He only laughed, because now they are numb and blind.
They tried to destroy him, break him down into ash.
But the lesson to learn was lost and he never looked back.

Flesh was only a casing that kept him under-wraps.
Now he wakes in the graveyard and Satan begins to laugh.
No one knows the outcome because now they all are dead.
So your one lesson lost, and he never looked back.

We the People

We the people, the freaks that the world casts away.
We the demons, mocking all of their pointless mistakes.
We the answer, as to why the darkness feels so cold.
We the monsters, here to feed on their very souls.

We are nothing that we weren't from the start.
You are nothing more to us than a senseless scar.
We are fighting to be free in this world that they made.
You are going to die if you don't get out of our way.

We the people, the ones who stand on edge looking down.
We the demons, laughing as all the world begins to drown.
We are the answer, as to why in darkness you feel so alone.
We are the monsters, that dwell within your very souls...

Hooks Through the Skin

One light shining, in the middle of the room.
Three nails burning, hidden beneath a tooth.
Nine cuts in the center and only dust bleeds out.
Hooks through the skin, pulling my muscles out.

Fate gave a notion, now pain is all I love.
Death has spoken, so what more can I give up?
Reason never mattered, so we jumped anyway.
Agony between two friends, insanity no longer insane.

One candle burning, lighting this broken room.
Three needles left inside, infecting both me and you.
Nine cuts in the center and only ashes bleed out.
Hooks through the skin, lifting me above the clouds...

MediEvil

Hammers beating me harder against all that was once real.
This heart torn from inside and the wound will never heal.
What were you saying? I don't think I heard it clear.
So why now are we fading and why don't you care?

Years have been taken, all now stands broken and in shame.
Timeless torment taking its toll on this life that can't be saved.
Medieval minds are breaking, all that you once held.
Why my love are you laughing, as we fall deeper into hell..?

Blades have been sharpened and now you test their strength.
What was I to you and who were you to me?
The logic of the blister has already done its time.
I don't want to lose you again but you already said goodbye...

182

Kiss Me With Hate

Go right ahead my love and do what you do best.
Take my hand and guide me, far beyond this life of stress.
Let us take a chance and try it - living a life of peace.
Kiss me again my love and watch this dreamer scream.

Lift it above your head now my love.
This heart as black as the tar that fills these lungs.
Go ahead and throw me back before this all is done.
So sorry if I wasn't there for you, so sorry the demon won.

Go right ahead my love and do what ever it is you wish.
Take my eyes out now and guide me into the abyss.
Let us take a chance and try it – living a life of peace.
Kiss me with hate my love and watch this dreamer weep.

Burning These Nerves

Baptize me in the flames and watch it purify my soul.
Lay me to sleep in the furnace so I can dream with the coals.
Drive the emotion within this spirit of now it's gotten too dark.
Love me the way you once did, then open my shallow scars.

Speak to me once again my lord, please save me from myself.
Take me far beyond the door, and show me a better hell.
Lie to me again, because the dream is where I fell in love with you.
Leave me beneath the flames, so I can burn numb just like you.

Baptize me in the pit of flames and watch it purify this soul.
Take me one step over and leave me eternally cold.
Drive the emotions bleak and kill what ever was.
Burn these nerves because you love me and leave me forever numb.

A State of Terror

Misguided attempts of taking back that only desire.
The time when I knew what it was that my heart did yearn.
Unmistakable, yet still lost far within a maze of my own fears.
Lusting a demon in spite, only to realize - no one cared.

What was it in the air that night, that made my eyes burn?
The blade shoved into my back so far, now it's stabbing my heart.
I wanted only to see one step further than the sight now unseen.
But reality has beaten me down once more and *you stole away my dream.*

Misguided attempts of taking my life back for myself.
Now passion has turned to poison and I can no longer breathe.
Unmistakable, yet I know in the end that you were nothing to me.
Lost in a state of terror, forever laughing because.
"This dreamer now - will never find sleep."

Shelter Me Again

What will it take to make all my memories just die?
As I step over the edge now and kiss this world goodbye.
All the demons of my past, now they start to laugh.
Because in the end I was only a freak from Hell.

My love - I guess she took my heart and threw it away.
In the end though, it was probably the only way.
What was the reason as to why I must burn like this?
So I take this rose now and hide it just beneath my wrist.

Darkness floods it still, the valley where no soul belongs.
Yet I wait here for hours, singing all my pointless songs.
Please shelter me from sin, and let me know release.
I never wanted to hurt anyone, but it's now too late for me.

So what will it take to make all my memories just die?
I truly don't want you to see this, so please close your eyes.
I've felt cold, for years I've been decaying within.
You cannot save me this time my love - *"you cannot shelter me again."*

Blood For Blood

The moonlight speaks to me still, so quiet and calm.
As all the thoughts bring on a chill, something has gone wrong.
The moments collapse, breaking down on my spine.
Their words have pushed me too far, so now it is time...

For every time they had pushed us down when we were down.
They must pay for creating the death of this world.
For every time they raised our hopes then let us fall.
They will burn for killing our innocent souls.

Blood tastes so sour when it's been spilt on the floor.
Someday you'll understand, what was behind that open door.
For now you must reap, that which you have sown.
An eye for an eye, blood for blood and no mercy on your souls.

Never Mine

That face, it was her smile that drove me insane.
That laugh, it was her laughter that caused me to collapse.
Those eyes, it was her eyes that gazed into my soul.
Those tears, it was her cries that killed me inside - *so now I am cold.*

Red – it was lying there, spread across the floor.
White – there was nothing I could do, to stop the snow.
Reason – there was no reason, for what I said.
Forgiveness – I will never forgive myself, for what I did.

That face, she was the angel that gave me sight.
That laugh, it was her smile that gave me life.
Those eyes, it was her eyes that gazed into my soul.
Those tears, it was her cries that burned me inside.
"But the Devil laughs, because she was never mine."

A Broken Creed

You took me too far out, into the sea of lasting fears.
Into the death of a bitter conscience, hidden behind those sad tears.
You lied to me once, when I was willing to accept whatever you'd say.
I loved once one of heaven's angels, but you took it away.

A line was drawn when you kept insisting on disrespect.
Logic pointed towards escape but you stayed here instead.
No one will save you now, because you've burned every last bridge.
You've crossed the line for the last time, so now this is it...

You pushed me too far, when you pushed the ones who were weak.
Into death you now go, and receive no pity from me.
You've taken God's words and set now a broken creed.
May our lord have mercy - when the two of you meet.

Dark Within This Heart

These arms reached out, hoping there is something to find.
Nothing in this dead space, only me and endless time.
Voices scream against me, from far inside my head.
No one can save me now, no one ever really tried...

These lives left bitter, I wish I had something more to say.
My mouth now broken, my thoughts left astray.
My only true passion was, the pain of you and me.
But now I am blind in this abyss, screaming with only me.

My hands reached out, sliding them across the floor.
I can feel nothing at all, nothing moves me anymore.
The voices sing louder, echoing from far inside.
But it's too dark within this heart, my soul is now blind.

Bleed Me to Life

Slit open my wrist and take a look inside.
Was I a great love to you or just a clown to pass your time?
Cut open my eyes to bleed out all that I have seen.
Watch me fail once more so you can all laugh at me.

Is it a masochist's dream to lie bleeding in this pool?
The day I gave you my heart is when I accepted being a fool.
Now nauseous as all that I was bleeds out onto the ground.
For what sin did I commit, as now to my fate I am bound.

Slit open my wrist and reach far inside.
Take out all that you can and sell it for a dime.
Cut open my eyes to bleed out all that I've once seen.
Bleed me to life or just leave me be...

Her Lips On My Tongue

She places her lips on my tongue to let me know she's awake.
She runs her fingers through my hair just to know that she's safe.
Her lasting wish was always to wake and look me in the eyes.
To see her smile again, would bring joy to my life.

She takes my hand when we stroll through the park.
She holds me as close as she can when it starts to get dark.
Her one lasting wish was to give me that kiss, as the sunset fades.
To be there at her side is all my heart truly wishes today.

She places her lips on my tongue to let me know she's there.
She kisses my neck as she runs her fingers through my hair.
Our only true hope, was that we would be together always.
So I place my finger over her lips because this dream could never be...

Murdering Dreams

Orchids fill these lungs as now the smoke fades.
All the little monsters have now come home to play.
But mother never wanted me to see passed my own eyes.
So she ripped them out and forever now I am blind.

Inside the sink is where I left those photos burning.
Because I cannot keep my heart from yearning her touch.
My love left me standing, out cold in the rain.
But nothing really matters anymore – only this eternal pain.

What rules you further than pride and pleasure?
Why am I damned for being a man of faith?
Mother never wanted me to grow, so she sawed off both my legs.
There is now nothing you can do, to save me from these aches.

Cyanide Cocktail

The salt grips me harder when the drink reaches the bottom.
No one can match what has become of this man.
All that ever stood for justice and eternal peace.
It is painted over and we're now forever lost.

I am no longer what you wanted me to be, "*and I do apologize for that.*"
I am not the child you knew anymore, "*I am the demon - now a man.*"
There never was a motive for you, only spite of what you are.
Still I sink beneath the drink, taking all my actions "*one step too far.*"

The shattered remains of what was once my face.
You cannot put the puzzle together without the missing piece.
All the flames that remain, they're burning loud within my heart.
Nothing now can save us my love, so take a drink with me and let us enjoy the burn.

Rushing Needles

There they go, watch them drift further inside.
Can you see the steam rising off my troubled eyes?
Where are all the smiles and why did they all break?
Here we go again, I hope it's not too late.

Watch as all the needles rush deeper into my spine.
Laugh at all the nonsense that bleeds from my mind.
So where are we all going, I hope we get there soon.
Please tell me that I mattered, at least to me and you.

There they go rushing, watch them sink inside.
Was there ever a justified reason or are we all just that blind?
Laugh a little louder so maybe God could hear.
Watch as they inject my heart, with all the angel's tears...

Dream Nothing

Dream the dreams of dying grace.
All I ever loved about you – now it dissipates.
All there ever was to say, I think it's all gone away.
Sorry for always being right, so I guess - I'll hit the lights...

The lies are building over the years.
The world is drowning in all her tears.
I hope you'll maybe start thinking straight.
If it's too much to ask, then I was truly too late.

Now that that was all said.
I think I would rather just be dead.
So maybe now you'll get your way.
As I dream nothing and you do the same.

Painted as Human

The canvas spoke the riddle that dug to the bone.
So please my love, don't leave me alone.
Yet no one's here as I begin to break.
Is this a punishment for one of my mistakes?

The ink still shapes me, because I am only a page.
The paint you hold will soon start to fade.
All my worries are slowly becoming facts.
So I begin to smile as I reach for the ax.

Nerves have lied to me for the very last time.
So slowly I begin to pull all the needles from my mind.
Yet you paint me as human, just to make yourself feel clean.
You know that you can never erase me, and you will never be free...

Coming Clean

Justify the filth and all the insects that are covering me.
Is it too much to bear, to watch the roaches infesting me?
Cut me open and let all the poison bleed out.
Stand back for a moment, as the snakes exit my mouth.

The sun is baking the dirt and grime onto my face.
So maybe now you'll recognize disgrace.
The wishes are failing because we've lost our faith.
The sludge is dripping but won't go away.

The fire can't clean it, all the sins that build onto me.
My fingers are broken, my eyes can no longer see.
There's no way now that you can stop the decay.
I'm coming clean so you'd better stay away.

Left There Standing

Rain drops beating, like needles ripping away my flesh.
A tattoo that remains forever, scarring me till death.
Frozen alone in the morning, knowing I can't find my way.
Still I wander lost, left there standing in the rain.

She was cold that night, the one that *never was...*
I was lost within myself, still lost forever without any luck.
She said she was happy that I showed up that night.
God please kill me, get me out of this life!

Time can't heal it, so I laugh and load the gun.
As I dance here alone, I remember what I've done.
I'll never forgive me, I'll never be fixed.
I was left there standing, so *"Always & Forever"* her smiles I will miss.

Jaded Oak

In both my hands I hold her name.
But still I weep and laugh in shame.
The taste of the razor was too much for me.
Now I'm gone and will never be seen.

Her thoughts were aching as were mine.
My body was freezing so she caught me on fire.
The last point was taken when I died on that day.
God won't forgive me but it's really okay.

In both my hands I hold her name.
It was so beautiful when she embraced me.
But now it's time again to let the credits roll.
I loved her to death and now she holds my soul...

Silly Pains

It tickles at first, before it sets in.
All that we said and all that we did.
The visions have pushed me too far today.
But still I laugh at all these silly pains.

Our words were flowing yet making no sense.
All the emotions I held for you, are all now spent.
The only true notion was set aside that day.
And still you question me, over all those silly pains.

It tickles at first but then starts to burn.
Maybe someday far from now, we both might learn.
Because nothing can change it or make it go away.
Yet still I'm laughing, at all these silly pains.

Smoke the Bullet

Take me riding, and place those razors beneath my eyes.
Rip me open my love, just to waste your time
The train is coming but it won't stop here today.
What will I do, when all the ghosts just fade away?

Watch me reach back and pull your knife from my spine.
Then I shove it as deep as I can, behind my left eye.
The only true motive was taken when you walked away.
God take me with you when you erase my tainted faith.

Hold me closer, because I can't stop shaking now.
If you ever truly cared for me, then please get me out.
The smoke is rising and it won't stop until we are gone.
So I smoke the bullet gone, hoping it won't take long...

Of-All-Now-Gray

Sometimes the hours seem to get longer every day.
But if I think about it hard enough it's still all the same.
Sometimes the smoke bleeds from all my open wounds.
You can't save me this time, this torment you just can't undo.

It drops further down, the blade that scrapes at my mind.
You laugh because I'm just a heartless clown, slowly biding its time.
Our natures keep us apart yet our souls desire each other.
I want only to hold her close again, but we are gone now – gone forever.

Sometimes the bones hurt as you pull them from beneath the skin.
But we both laugh because it's all happening again.
The last purpose given, when we decided to walk away.
I want to tell her the reason I love her yet, of-all-now-gray.

Midday

I wasn't ready to be put through this test.
I just can't stop it now, it's far too late to protest.
I want to get out and stop beating myself to death.
Why can't God just forgive me, like he did all the rest?

It's getting darker now, but I'm not ready to see the light.
Why didn't you warn me, why must it always be a fight?
You could have told me, that it would come down to this.
Please wait a moment, and just let me catch my breath.

I wasn't ready to be put through this pain.
I can't believe that you just stood there laughing at me.
I want some answers and to just wake up at home.
But the time has come and yes, "I am alone..."

Chapter 11

One Day

Uno Mas

One more time the needles fall deep within.
Pushing at the back of my eyes, erasing all I ever did.
One more scream and all we ever hoped for was lost.
In the end I knew I loved you but that line was already crossed.

One more fable and then we must let the credits roll.
Watch as our failing dreams give birth to another sad ghost.
One more bad drink just to get us through the day.
Warm as it pours down, filling our hollow graves.

One more loss of rights and then we have the right to react.
Please wait here as I pull slowly, your knife from my back.
One more time, I had let my pride control who I am.
One more time I bury myself beneath the dust, blood and ash.

Apathy

Timeless waiting for hope at the end of the hall.
Watching as all that I ever cared for slowly begins to fall.
Laughing as they take my words and rip them from my head.
Now walking away - before there is none of me left.

Reaching into the back of the notebook trying to find a page.
Pulling back only ashes that I brought from her grave.
Knowing that it's over and it has still yet to begin.
Now I take another step knowing that soon this road must end.

Watching the people around me indulge themselves day to day.
Laughing as they burn forever over all their pointless mistakes.
I'm taking in all the sights of the world as it fails before my eyes.
Still I'm laughing as they waste all their meaningless lives.

Timeless trying to make sense of the screams that echo inside.
Watching as my loved ones fade because they were never really alive.
Taking another step passed all that we strived for in our time.
Now walking away from the world because I never cared for its lies.

Starving

The hunger sets in again and I can't see passed my own eyes.
This body begins to shake as this heart starts to writhe.
Nothing can stop it, or give satisfaction to what I crave.
Please run now my love, hurry and get away.

The hunger has set in again and I can't judge reality anymore.
This body has changed again, as my thoughts lie dead on the floor.
I can't be held reasonable for the actions that occur from this point on.
I've given you fair warning, so your hopes are all null and void.

The hunger has set in once again and I can't stop it this time.
This body is starving so I hope I gave you enough time.
Nothing can stop it now, please just run and escape.
I shall never stop feeding until you satisfy what I crave.

Love Lost Meaning

It tickles a bit, the blade pushing at the back of my heart.
What truly was the meaning and why did I fail from the start?
I've taken my time and tried to let all my emotions go.
Now that you're here again my heart no longer knows.

The pictures on the walls seem to bare no color anymore.
The music rings numb as I lie naked on the floor.
All the sweet things we said have been forgotten with time.
So I sit here alone in darkness, watching myself unwind.

It was funny at first, now I don't think the joke makes any sense.
So here we go once more and I guess that's what I get...
It's starting to hurt, that blade pushing from my back and against my heart.
So love lost its meaning and neither of us learned.

Just Waiting

I am a lost cause, just waiting to lose.
I am beneath the frost, just waiting for winter to bloom.
I was a man once, just waiting for his chance.
I am now a mistake, just waiting to forget its past.

I am a monster, just waiting for its birth.
I am a ghost now, just waiting for remorse.
I am forgotten, just waiting to be known.
I am a dreamer, just waiting to go home.

I am a lover, just waiting to find love.
I am an angel, just waiting to see above.
I am a failure, just waiting to fail.
And I am a demon, just waiting for hell.

Bleed Outside the Circle

This trip has worn my soul down to its core.
But if I think real hard, I never had time for your chorus.
It pulls to the right and goes for miles until it turns.
Then we're back where we started, so never will we learn.

The tide has gone out and I don't think it's coming back.
Our time has run out, so please tell death to take me back.
I've asked nothing more, than to burn the flesh off these bones.
My love you never cared, so please just leave me alone.

It's darker now, because you've reached in and stolen my eyes.
Do you feel colder now? Maybe someday we'll understand why.
The moon whispers again but says nothing that I didn't know.
My love you never cared for me, so as I bleed outside the circle.
"Just leave me alone..."

Remnants

My head feels heavy as if it weighs a ton.
The smoke won't leave so it floods both my lungs.
My arms are tired and can't hold a thing.
My legs are giving out, so maybe I'll just stay.

Down on the ground I watch the blood pour from my mouth.
I try to speak to God but nothing seems to come out.
Pain echoes and reminds me that I'm not dead yet.
But these voices inside have other plans for my death.

So what is left now, other than me?
The thought of holding on is now beginning to leave.
I watch all the pieces of my heart lie steaming on the floor.
As I spit out the last chunk it feels cold to the core.

So what did you want from me, other than my life?
What now is left of me, just a waste of God's time...?
Broken and I am the last one left who cared.
Just one more piece taken, then we're left with only despair.

The Struggle Beyond

It pushes only to see what could happen if it reacts.
You push me only to see what would happen if I come back.
The starlight illuminates no further than here.
Push all you wish but you'll soon get what you fear.

The tearing inside and leaving only regret.
Run all you want but you'll soon be out of breath.
I've seen how the story ends but I won't let you know.
And still you try to see what I've hidden behind my soul.

It takes some time to understand what it means to feel loss.
You push me still just to see what would happen if I lost.
The last hope you had was to just leave me alone in shame.
But now that I've seen you, you are the one to blame.

Days That Meant So...

There was once a time when all I had was you.
The days when we smiled and rejoiced in our youths.
We would hold each other's hands and walk through the park.
So please tell me why, does today feel so dark..?

There was once a time when I enjoyed a kiss that felt so real.
I held her in my arms for hours keeping my heart still.
We would laugh over nothing and smile everyday.
So please tell me why, am I alone in this grave..?

There were those days that meant so much to both her and me.
The time when we would make love and set our minds free.
We knew in our hearts that those emotions would last forever.
But tomorrow has come and gone as I lie alone in this graveyard.

Her Laughter Rings

Her laughter rings still so many years passed.
I've reached so hard but still can't pull the knife from my back.
Her smile haunts me, she wants me to feel so cold.
I've tried all I can to forget her, so now I am truly alone.

Her laughter rings on, tormenting my troubled brain.
I've taken matters into my own hands so now you will see.
Her words meant so much once when I held her in my heart.
But I've taken it out now and tore it apart.

There's no time left for me, to tell you what I mean.
She was just an angel that once got the best of me.
Her laughter rings on, and on and on until death.
But now that this gun is loaded, maybe I can get the last laugh...

Miscellaneous

So many things I've yet to say to you my love.
What of all the times when we were the ones who touched.
Now all that's left of the memory is a collective book of pain.
All I can hold of you now, is bloody teeth and that ring.

What of all the words we said when the lights were off.
What now can I do to melt away the eternal frost?
So many things between you and me have still gone on unsaid.
Why God does it hurt so, when I begin to turn my head?

So I'm nothing now and never truly was a thing.
So we're over now, it's been years and I still feel the sting.
So much building inside of my skull, "I think it's gonna break."
And still there's so much my love, that I have still yet to say.

All-Ready

The leash has been tightened and I want only to be held.
Why must you beat me – why will no one help?
The lecture was given but I just couldn't hear a thing.
And all over again I know, that I'm left with only me...

The birds are flocking away with a fear of things to come.
I wish I could follow but these wings have come undone.
The wolf just waits there but someday it might react.
I'm just sitting here alone, licking the rusted blade of the ax.

Words seem so pointless when no one's there to hear a thing.
Again I see the outline of all the troubles yet to be.
There was once an outlet that I strived for everyday.
But once more I realize that I just can't be saved.

The leash has been tightened and I just want to be held.
Why must you hate me – why must I lie alone in hell?
There's nothing left to reach me, I'm on the edge looking down.
It's time again to see the end "*so if we're all ready,*" let's end it now...

March of the Ants

There they go, marching into the back of my brain.
It stirs up the voices and now they won't sleep.
The ants are taking all that I once was in the past.
Please just end me and destroy my last breath.

The ants are flooding me and I just laugh at the pain.
Blood now is just a sip of last night's hollow drink.
There they go, marching on until the job is done.
So I take one of the ants and load him into my gun.

The queen gave her command and now the ants are here.
I guess I deserve it all so I need not to fear.
What ever was the meaning, they do not say.
The ants march on, taking me so very far away...

You Were There...

The clouds rolled in and it seemed like a sad dream.
Darkness flooded the town and I began to hear the screams.
The moon smiled at me yet it was the middle of the day.
I could only laugh because it was the end – of all things to be...

The lost notions were pushing hard, trying to get their say.
But no one was left to care, they all just went away.
Silence began to pound against my heart because I was so scared.
Death stood there waiting as the smoke filled the air.

The clouds rolled in and they felt like a heavy dust and ash.
Darkness flooded the town but there was no one left to look back.
The moon came closer and kissed me on the cheek because I was scared.
Death stood there waiting and yes, you were there...

Am I Insane?

No one to confide in, only the walls and the screams.
No one's here to hear me, yet still I begin to sing.
The faces of past monsters begin to paint themselves on the floor.
And mother won't wake me, because she doesn't care anymore.

Food tastes so tasteless and water has turned to ash.
I can feel only the chill of darkness, the flames no longer react.
Touch seems so distant, because no one's here to feel my face.
Life seems so lifeless, so why must I sit here and wait?

Nothing moves me any further than the middle of me.
Still I hope and pray that this is but only a sad dream...
The faces speak in voices that only my heart can hear.
Yet I've become deaf, when my love, she ate away all my cares.

No one to confide in, only the stains on the walls and sheets.
I can no longer read the writing, it's all just Greek to me.
So am I insane, as I lie here cold and naked weeping on the floor?
No one will save me now, because you don't care anymore.

The One With Fear

The hallway seems so long, miles until the end.
Yet they sent me down, to be judged for all my sins.
As it takes days until I reach, I have the time to slowly think.
Of all the times I enjoyed hurting you.

The doors are all locked and I cannot turn back now.
It's still so many miles until the end, God help me now!
So was I the one who pushed the button and watched as we all died?
Was I the one just laughing, as the angel began to cry?

The end seems to get further with every step I take.
But I can't give up now, it is far too late.
So was I the one who enjoyed feasting upon all your sad tears.
No – I was just the child who lived his life in fear...

Between (Myself & Me)

I can't fight it any longer, the time is now and now we act.
I can't be the one you hate, I cannot be the only one left.
We can't just fake it and try to say that it meant something more.
We cannot stay here, soon they'll shut and lock the door.

I can't be pushed into doing something, that I know is wrong.
I can't be pressured, so I won't go along.
We can't just sit here and let this war destroy our lives.
We cannot just forgive and forget, we must stand up with pride.

I can't see it anymore, the blood has stained the mirror with shame.
I can't fight it anymore, I must pay for all my mistakes.
We can't just fake it, we must accept all outcomes to be.
So I will fight on in this war between, "*Myself & Me.*"

Was I That Evil?

You look at me with a face of both pity and shame.
A look of disappointment when you see the scars on my face.
So who were you to me and was I the one who cared?
Where did all the emotions go, they must've turned to air.

Was I that evil, did I laugh at you when you were down?
Was I that heartless, did I encourage you and then cast you out?
Were we great friends or lovers that always tried?
Was I that evil, did I laugh as you cried?

Am I that monster, the one you hate and fear?
Give me please a reason, as to why we no longer care.
So was it our passion that drove us deep into hell?
Was I truly that evil, when I laughed as you fell...?

Yet To Come

Yet to come and yet to go.
Miles to walk, so far to the unknown.
Days to lose and hours to waste.
As all our dreams simply begin to fade.

Forced to try and damned to lose.
All the secrets, hidden in front of me and you.
Lives to save and hearts to break.
Pushing and pushing harder against the grain.

Yet to come and yet to go.
All the things in life we'll just never get to know.
Days to wait and hours now gone.
Someday you'll see, that we were both wrong.

Seen It Ten Times

Like a tornado tearing inside of my aching mind.
I can no longer focus, I think I've gone blind.
The answers are swinging about, right in front of our face.
We try to reach out but fall short of length.

Proud of the fact that we still call this our home.
Yet I'm still here inside weeping - so dark and alone.
The acid has taken all that it can take today.
So if you have the time, please find me my face...

Like a bad joke gone good, still it hurts at the start.
If you're nice to me now, I'll let you feel all my scars.
I've seen it before, the shadow that calls itself me.
And even now I laugh, as I watch the mirror scream.

Don't Say

Don't say to me, that I wasn't a great chapter in your life.
Don't act as if, things weren't great when we turned off the lights.
You were the reason, as to why my mind aches at night.
You were the only thing I had, in this sad and tormented life.

Don't say that you're sorry, not after you laughed at me.
Don't say it was nothing, because it meant the world to me.
Time has taken, and now all that I was has already passed.
Pain has now awakened, so be ready for the last act.

Don't say that you love me, because I know that's a lie.
Don't say that you're lonely, just open your eyes.
Don't say that I'm the bad guy, because I know that's a fact.
And don't say that you cared, because you've never looked back.

Just Like You

Pain fills this body when she smiles at me.
The words can't seem to surface so I try not to speak.
She knows that I'm standing here, waiting for a sign.
But she just smiles because she knows that I'm right.

Pain boils inside me when she says that I'm the one who's bad.
My thoughts begin to splinter so I rip them from my head.
She said that she would be there but I stood waiting all day.
But she was always with me, always and a day.

Pain rules out reason when she touches my face.
I want only to tell her, but the words all just fade.
She knows that I'm standing there waiting for a sign.
And it's just like you to say, that everything is going to be fine...

As Everyone Else

As everyone knows, this war has just only begun.
As still the bastard laughs, reloading his gun.
It feels so jaded, victory can never be found.
And on we battle until all the motives begin to drown.

As everyone knows, I've yet to reach that goal that I seek.
But someday I might realize that it's always been in front of me.
It seems so faded, the thought that I might smile today.
I thought about it once but then it went away.

As everyone knows, she was happy once – with me.
It's been years now, so maybe it was all just a dream.
It's like no one cares anymore about this hollow man's cries.
And as everyone else knows, it's all just a matter of time...

Someone In the Mirror

It took me awhile, but I think it's going to be okay.
It's darker now, yet I can't find any shade.
The words were spoken, but she never cared for me.
My thoughts are all broken, as I stand forever apart from me.

It took me awhile, but now the ashes have filled these lungs.
I stand here alone again, laughing as I load the gun.
It's funny to me, that I just can't see a thing.
The voices ring on, but still I feel the scream.

It took me awhile, but now I think it's all clear.
The years of bleeding for nothing and waiting alone in fear.
Someone's out there, trying to see beyond my tears.
Someone's waiting for me, someone in the mirror.

On the Mattress

Constant ripping, the thorn from my spine.
Still you stand there, telling me to just give it time.
I want this right now, I don't have the time to wait.
Let's do this right now, then we'll clean off the slate.

Constant pulling, taking out that remaining thread.
Still you stand there, telling me it's all in my head.
I want you right now, you know you want me too.
Let's get this over with, then we can start over anew.

Constant hitting, against this skull goes more rage.
Still you hate me, but it's all the very same.
I need you right now, lie on the mattress and close your eyes.
Let's do this right now, then we'll both see the light.

What's Out There?

The roads seem as if they are my only friends.
Time and time again, they comfort me with the soothing winds.
The roads seem as if, they are the only ones who care.
Miles and miles I go, wondering what's out there...

The sun beats down harder, but the roads keep me aware.
The flesh on my feet is gone, but I don't seem to care.
The moon kisses me, as the stars guide my way.
Sometimes I wonder what's out there, beyond the oceans and seas.

The roads keep me going, pain has now become my bride.
The roads love me forever, the roads give me the time.
Miles and miles I go, but I just truly don't care.
On I wander and wonder, "What's really out there...?"

Shaving It Close

Take me with you God, when all the fires burn out.
Hold me close Satan, and let's watch as the angels shout.
It's funny now, because we knew this day would come.
You're laughing again, but it might be over done.

Take me home when the credits roll.
I want to be in bed, when it all starts crashing down.
Show me a better way, and then there just might be another way out.
Laugh my love, lost lonely and leaving it all in the grave.

Take me with you God, when the final song begins to play.
Hold me closer Satan, before it all just fades away.
It's coming now and we laugh because we know it's here.
We shaved it a little too close this time, so today it rains the angel's tears.

Up Here

Up here the air gets thin and we can barely breathe.
Up here we are alone, where no one can hear you scream.
Up here is where I go to escape it all and see the light.
Up here is where I'm waiting, waiting and waiting all night.

This is the place where all the monsters dream.
A sad yet colorful place that seems odd yet free.
Pain is the water we drink and in blood we bathe.
This is the place I go, to just simply get away.

Up here the stars are almost close enough to grab.
Up here we all enjoy the pleasures of constant gab.
Up here is where I go to leave your troubled world behind.
Up here is where I'm waiting, waiting and waiting for the right time.

210

Sleepless Screams

Sleepless screaming, lifeless dreaming.
Wishing there was a better way out of this hell.
Hopeless waiting, heartless breaking.
Knowing that in the end, nothing will help.

Time has forced me to push against the grain once again.
So I have no choice but to laugh as you pay for all your sins.
It's just so funny to me that we were never free.
So why did we fight if it was only to fail...?

Sleepless screaming, timeless dreaming.
Wishing that I would just escape my own head.
Hopeless tearing, no one is caring.
Maybe it would hurt a little more if I wasn't already dead.

Hour 25

The sands of time have now created a prison of stone.
My head full of laughter, as I lie here all alone.
It seems funny to me, that I still can't see my own face.
But in the end, this smile I would never replace.

Father-Time is now done playing his games with my heart.
But still it hurts, as I stare up at the stars.
Passion feels so pointless, it breaks me down when I try.
So I wait here all day, for hour 25.

The sands of time, they flood my tired soul.
Ages come and gone, so now it feels so cold.
I've yet to see myself happy, though I know I've tried.
So on and on I wait here, for hour 25...

Chapter 12

My Rotting Muse

Leading Lunatics

Lifeless laughter left leading lunatics lost.
Head slammed against a bullet, because we never cared for the cost.
It hurts so much, knowing my nerves don't work any more.
But still life seems funny to me, now that I'm a corpse.

Hopeless heartache heeding our last breath.
It takes so much of me, now I don't think there will be anything left.
It seems darker now, the sun has gone black and I slowly begin to laugh.
We've come so far in this war but I don't think they'll ever look back.

Worst was what we worried when waging war within.
It seems as if all the emotions I held for you have now become sins.
As it breaks in deeper and the screaming drowns out all the tears.
We're left leading lunatics again, as they wait for us in the mirror.

Where Did it Get Me?

In the end of all things to be, where did it ever truly get me?
In the end of the story that no one will ever read.
Tell me why must this dreamer never find sleep?
In the end of all things yet to come, tell me when will it all be done...?

Seven years spent and gone so what have I left now!?
A small pill hidden beneath my tongue, just to get me out.
Nine times against the brick and now it shatters under the skin.
I crawl under the flesh of the demon just to find my name once again.

In the end of the lie that mother gave when we were born.
Now truth slams us down, bringing on a raging storm.
So tell me why did I fight this war, if only to lose my love and heart.
So where did it get me, all the years of pains and scars...?

Because You Worried

A mile down, but no one will be there when we hit.
Too far out, so does God know when the voices will quit?
It's a stranger act, the rusted thought of when I looked back.
So get me out, show me pity behind all your words of doubt.

The last time I tried, it felt like razors behind my eyes.
Now the walls are speaking the lyrics soft, so listen close.
Alone in the hallway I wonder, how long have I been a ghost?
The vibrations ringing as the whispers are singing, *me deeper into hell.*

Because you worried, all our dreams came to a miserable end.
Now within the blood I pay, for each and every pointless sin.
The torment was and will always be the only truth in my life.
Because you worried, now in darkness I close my eyes.

One Mile to Home

The roads have melted with time, now just tar and sand.
All the beasts of the world are dead, just dust and ash.
The words were spoken, but no one's left to hear it ring.
All the clouds have fallen from the sky, as have the Devil and I.

No one's here now to see what goes on when the lights go out.
No one's here to see, what has become of all our dreams.
It's over now, all the cards have just been played.
It's all gone, just rust remains in our futile graves.

One mile to home, but maybe that's not where I should be.
Why did I remain, tell me why is it only me?
The passion of failure has stained our meaningless slate.
Just one more mile, then all will fade.

A Struggle to See

I believe that God cares when we fall from the path.
I believe it matters to the Devil if we never look back.
But someone tell me why, is it just so hard to step away.
Why is it when all is over, we begin to accept our mistakes.

A heartbeat misses and you start to know something's wrong.
When the music begins to play, just try to sing along.
Because it's a struggle to see beyond all the lies and pains.
It was just a life of grief, but we lived it anyway.

Pain was there for us, when we just needed to pass some time.
When our lips pressed together the Gods labeled it as a crime.
So on we follow, hoping we'll awake at the end of the ride.
But it's a struggle to see, when God has taken our eyes...

Betrayed For What?

She smiles when I tell her she's all I've ever loved.
She places her hand on my shoulder taking my heart above.
But then the clouds cover over and time begins to slow.
No words seem to surface, so I lie alone beneath the snow.

She smiles when I'm looking but I know she's mad when I turn away.
She laughs with a scream, as she begins to betray.
No lines to keep us together, so I guess I have nothing to say.
But it's still so funny to me, that I'm still lying awake.

She said that I was the only, true love in her life.
But why does my back still hurt, maybe it's her rusted knife.
So why is it, that I just can't seem to get a break...?
And for what damn reason, have I once again been betrayed?

"So it is true, that my heart is dead..."

Senseless Falling

Colorful lights bending at the edge of the blade.
A noose left hanging as the bastard slowly waits.
Time no longer matters because we don't have the *time* to care.
And now we begin to fall, only to see if death is there...

A broken life left losing all chances of knowing why.
Then it begins to bleed out, the needles from these eyes.
But no one waits to see it, the man without a face.
So now we plummet again, a thousand miles below our graves.

Justice never concerned itself, so what was the point?
You can't see the right answers anymore, so you call it null and void.
It's just so senseless now, to care for a soul that is lost.
So I smile with a laugh, as we all begin to fall.

A Time For Rest

So heavy – so heavy – so heavy.
The screws tighten against the bones to keep it straight.
What was the motive then and was it all just a mistake?
Tell me I matter to you now because I don't think I do.
Take me when I'm gone, to the dark side of the moon.

So broken – so broken – so broken.
It crawls its way in and makes its home deep inside.
All the demons of this soul, maybe they've already died.
But how can I just say that it'll be alright someday.
I think I should just rest, before I begin to fade.

So lost – so lost – so lost.
Pain rises to the surface when the pills dissipate.
I want you to hold me when I go, but now it's too late.
We wish from time to time that our dreams could maybe come true.
But I think I should rest now, before I end up like you...

218

Cutting Slowly

The razor pushes down on the flesh separating smooth.
The razor pushes the flesh apart allowing blood to bloom.
I cut it slowly just to watch the blade sink into the skin.
I love the sight of the metallic - diving beneath the wrist.

The blade feels cold as it begins to break the surface.
Of all, it is this pain that I love the best.
I so love it as the skin pulls open and the bone is exposed.
I lick the blood off the meat and it tastes just so cold.

I guide it slowly across and now just little dots of red.
Tilted back and now it's wide open and inside I see what's left.
I love the thought of burning but only ice remains in this heart.
So still I'm cutting slowly, all my troubles apart.

Do You Agree?

I took my first step over and now I fall away.
I eat the flesh of my lover, just to forget her face.
The Devil laughs because I told him that I was taking his throne.
Now he's mad because I did and he's left all alone.

Mother said that she would be there no matter what the cost.
I've been waiting here forever, maybe she got lost.
Why am I still weeping, the dust from these eyes?
Why are we still laughing, at the child that went blind?

I feel that there's no winning, because this is not a game.
Will this story ever get better, or will it just stay the same?
But I know that we can make it if we try hard today.
But I guess the real question is, "do you agree?"

Same Page

Untold were the answers that you seek everyday.
Miles into hell, that might be where we should stay.
A song never sung but we know it in our souls.
As we follow on in this riddle that always seemed cold.

A life lead deeper into the hopes of her smile.
Now anger seems as our only choice in this chronicle of denial.
What would the purpose be for us to keep failing like this?
And on we go, another mile into the abyss.

Unseen are the truths that we fight for everyday.
So only to feel closer to home, we stick our heads in the flames.
It's all just a conundrum in a dream that never fades.
Although our lives may be different stories, it's still the same page.

Through the Rain

This room feels colder, the flickering lights are burning out.
This room seems stagnate, with lingering thoughts of doubt.
The hallway feels longer, as if it goes on and on for days.
The mirror looks dark, I can't even see my own face.

The rain is falling, as down this long hallway I stroll.
Now I understand what it means, to be soaked to the bone.
The rain is rising and still I see no end to my troubles in sight.
But all I truly want is for someone to turn off the lights.

This life seems colder, all the voices now feel sorry for what they said.
The world feels darker, maybe it's just because I'm already dead.
The hallway is so long now and the rain falls down over my head.
And still on I move, praying that someday the rain might end...

Get Me There!

Fingernails grinding deep beneath my flesh.
The last words of the dreamer are what our God loved best.
The action of ripping the cells out, of this twisted brain.
Some think it's excessive, others think it's insane.

So get me there now! And show me what I truly was.
Give me a better lie, then load it into this gun.
We're dancing everyday, a mile beneath the lake.
And no matter what they say, it was just so very fun.

Mnemophobic words were spoken but no one ever looked.
As now I hide this face, deep within that secret nook.
Just get me there and tell me what I was!
Why can't I be forgiven, for the one damned life I took?

Passion Beyond Feeling

Passion beyond feeling, words spoken without a mouth.
Lies that remain bitter, as they drill within leaving only doubt.
A love lost for ages, but she plagues this mind anyway.
Why do I act as if I have a heart, I know they took it away.

Reason flooding the thoughts, passion now forever lost.
Lives trying to stand firm in the light, this heart broken over time.
An action that they've forgotten, but I know that it was right.
Passion beyond feeling, death found without a life.

Demons feeding monsters, so cold in this shallow grave.
Miles towards what I've been seeking, and still so many years away.
Thoughts that meant so much then, but now they begin to break.
Felt passion beyond feeling, so this life was my only mistake.

Fear Because I Can

I'm not the one in charge, of why the waves push against the stone.
If you asked me now, I'd much rather be alone.
Pain fuels it still, and no matter what, I know I won't be saved.
I fear because I can, and I know that you feel the same.

It's growing in deeper, the last thing she said was true.
But I can't remember her face anymore, still my heart remembers the swoon.
So now it's over, as I lie broken here beneath the coals.
I'm not the one to blame for your misery, but still I know you do...

If you asked me now, I would tell you that we're out of time.
Still we move onward, following the shattered line.
Into death is where we head now, but someday we might be saved.
So I fear because I can, and know it will never change.

I've Seen An Angel

I've stepped upon the path that leads into the village called the *Unknown*.
Into the market I wonder, pondering what may lie within.
I've reached a place where I know might hold what I seek.
Only to find that no one can help me, I'm just another unseen.

I've taken a step upon the streets in the village called the *Unknown*.
Only to realize in spite of all my strives, I truly have no home.
I've looked far within the broken mirror hoping to see.
But after all of my battles, I am truly the unseen.

I've took another step towards whatever may lie ahead of me.
Then I came across an angel, dancing down by the stream.
I watched her dance and sing with such a beautiful smile on her face.
But not even the angel could see, "*this ghost*" forever disgraced.

The Stage Calls

Quiet – the floor seems faded, a darkened shade of green.
The walls are blank, nothing in the frames to see.
The faces gather around watching my soul bleed off my tongue.
As I spit out another lyric, I know that I am home.

Alone with a thousand faces gazing up at me.
In hell I burn still, knowing that I can't be free.
It's quiet now, but then the music starts to play.
And I can hear her calling, my love – the stage.

Alone – still hoping that the Devil will ease my troubled heart.
And I watch as the thousand zombies, begin tearing my brain apart.
No escape from this nightmare, as I look down and begin to sing.
Then only a smile, because this is right where I should be.

Fighting For the Right

I won't stand for this anymore, the way you make me feel.
I can't stand this anymore, this heart that won't ever heal.
I've lost all that could ever be, something wonderful in my life.
Now what can I do, to make amends for all our strives?

I'm fighting onward, praying that I might gain a ray of hope.
But now that I'm here I begin to feel the choke.
Because you never cared for me, it was all just a lie.
Now I'm left in constant pain, ever since I've opened my eyes.

The dawn has gone away, so what more now can I do?
You've left my heart astray, only for my hatred to bloom.
They've taken all that was once, my little world of peace.
Now I'm fighting for the right, to set this life free...

Wall of Faces

Stranger than the time when we both knew it was pain.
Now as the last drop boils, you try to look away.
For only now the Gods know, that we are here alive.
But they've all looked away, so forsaken we begin to cry.

The wall of faces speaks to me, *"again I ask its help."*
The wall gives a whisper, leading only into hell.
We've taken all we can, so now it's up to faith.
So I guess that's the only option, so now we step away.

It's stranger now, than the last time we both felt the sting.
Now as the last word is spoken, we laugh together and weep.
For what better reason did we have, and why now is it a mistake?
The wall of faces told me the truth, and I guess that's why you walked away.

The Clock That Cared

Strike another hour gone and now it decays away.
The life of a child gone, now only this demon remains.
A time when we were happy, I think it was all a lie.
But we tell it anyway, just to keep it alive.

The stone - it knew my name, *"is that why I feel so cold."*
The owl looked away, because it knows I don't have a soul.
The words have never changed, for some reason they're still here.
And through all of this pain, there was that one clock that cared.

Strike another year away and now those memories decay.
So the life we lived was only a dream that was taken away.
But I remember a time, when you were all that mattered to me.
So now that it's over and we know our time is near.

"Through all of the pain. Still I remember, that one clock that cared."

The Devil Demands

The Devil demands, that we should get ours while we can.
And take what ever we need, if right from their hands.
What motive more would we require, in this broken world of pain?
The Devil demands us to be happy, no matter what it takes.

This burning pain, it has gone numb and so have I.
The future seems faded, as I feel it behind my eyes.
The wrong words were spoken, and God just looked away.
The Devil demands that we should ask forgiveness and *admit to our mistakes.*

We are troubled little creatures, just scurrying on in our lives.
Hoping maybe we will hit it big, then waste it to the very last dime.
So what can we ask for, in this tormented world of rage?
The Devil demands us to find the answer, before it's too late.

Her Last Moment

She was waking, taking in a deep breath.
She was hoping, someone would answer her request.
The line was drawn, and it takes us way – way back.
She wanted just the world then, and to never give it back.

Her last words were that she was comfortable at the time.
All she ever wanted, was for me to burn alive.
She was awkward in her speech, but I knew what she meant.
So now that it's over, was any of it good time spent?

She was waking, taking in a tired breath.
She was hoping that I was gone, "so she was right I guess."
There was a line drawn once, but then it just turned to ash.
In her last moment she smiled - but then again, I never looked back.

What Family Have I?

What family have I to speak of? Mother just walked away.
What past have I to cherish? It was only a youth of pain.
What thoughts have I to remember? I think I just forgot.
What life have I to live? I guess I am truly lost...

What family have I to adore? As I wait here alone-broken on the floor.
What actions have I to act on? I'll just hope a better outcome today.
What love have I to hold now? She just threw me away.
What reason have I to move on? Maybe I should just stay.

What family have I to think of? No one's here with me now.
What more have I to find out? In this world of constant doubt.
What life have I to live now? It might be time to just admit I'm insane.
And what family have I to love now? They all just threw me away.

I Crawl Beneath

I crawl beneath, this very page that you read.
I'm lost beneath, all the thoughts you hold of me.
You can't make it change, so hopefully soon it'll go away.
I can't let it break, so now it's done and I simply fade.

I crawl beneath, the wound across your open wrist.
I'm lost behind, that one *unforgettable* kiss.
You can't make me take it away, so I left it in that grave.
I won't just let us break, but no matter what - I still begin to fade.

You took my heart, and now I have nothing inside but tar.
Now over and over in these lungs, you place your fingers over the scars.
We can't hide it anymore, now they know what we truly are.
So I crawl beneath, that very dream you hold of me.

Laughter Failed

This mask has a name that no one can bear.
Truth holds it forever, the thought of despair.
I can't let you out now, you've seen way too much.
I know that I'm joking, but you're still out of luck.

The ground is now quaking, I feel my heart breaking.
But no matter what, I know you don't care.
The world was a sad dream, that we all had one night.
But now that we're gone, nothing left here is alright.

This mask has a name that most don't want to hear.
Truth hides behind, every thought of fear.
But I just can't stand it, the fact that we are all in hell.
Well I guess we have to face the truth, that all our laughter has truly failed.

I Just Want to Feel Okay

All I want in this life, is to just feel okay.
But darkness bleeds out again, leaving a bloody stain.
The gravity of this moment, it's breaking apart my spine.
Reality has never felt this real, so it might just be a lie.

The ocean called for me, so now I sink below the waves.
Only to awake in a pool of blood, sweat, piss and pain.
But I just want to feel okay, in this sad dream called eternity.
But I know it won't happen, so what have I to say?

The only thing I have left, is a memory of when I was yours.
But I know now that I was used, and insanity took its course.
All I've ever wanted, was for us to just be happy and free.
But you hate me now and it's over, but I just want to feel okay...

Brain Grind

It's melting, the stem caught on the edge of the blade.
You're weeping, is it because I'm a monster without a face?
The Devil lusting, laughing at the fact of what we are.
Now we are drowning, in a pool of boiling tar.

The vibrations are pushing, I'm at the edge looking down.
So you all point and laugh, at this sad broken clown.
I've reached in deeper, but I only found blood and ash.
My heart has been taken, and never given back.

This heat is pulling me further, into the end of humanity's fears.
My spine is itching, so I pulled it out from behind the left ear.
I scratch as hard as I can, and it feels so good covered in lime.
This brain has had its time, so now we begin to grind...

I Give You My Face

My love, this gift is all I can afford now at this time.
Just this gift of my eternal love and pride.
You've taken my gift my love, but then you threw it away.
I have nothing else to offer, so am I to live forever disgraced?

Take it with you my love, this shell of a broken man.
Please hold me close and never let me fade again.
You've taken my gift my love, and I see a look of peace.
But again you cast me away my love, you only wish to erase me.

My love what can I do now, to show you how much I care.
I'll give all the blood I can bleed, "*I'll give my very last breath of air.*"
You've taken my vows my love but then you laughed and left me in pain.
You've destroyed all that I am, still I give to you this gift – "*my face...*"

Nameless You Fade

Who was the girl that was written about for so many years?
Who was the lover of the demon that bleeds frozen tears?
Who was the answer to the question of how and why?
Nameless you fade my love, lost forever in time.

Who was the woman that the poet obsessed over for years?
Who was the motive to all his lonely tears?
Who was the answer to the riddle of what it all meant?
Nameless you fade my love, gone forever in the abyss.

Who were we then my love and what have we become?
Who was the girl that remains etched in this book?
Who was the love - of the poet that refused to walk away?
Nameless you fade my love, erased forever from this brain.

Muse-less

I've done all I can, so now it's up to fate.
I've said all there is, that I've ever needed to say.
So what is there now, to shine me a better path?
But I know no matter what, I must never look back.

What is there left now, to fuel my troubled brain?
I think I've said enough now, so I guess I'll go away.
So is there any reason now, to look for a new view of faith?
Muse-less I wonder, why I can't just walk away.

I've done all I can, to not lose myself over the years.
But still I am drowning, in this red pool of my own tears.
I can't let you see me now, but you never did from the start.
So muse-less I wait, for a new faith beyond these scars.

Chapter 13

Behind Open Doors.

Psycho-Logical

It pushes us further, all the moments when we were one.
It takes us further, all the times we loaded the gun.
So it brings us down, to a level that we've never tried.
So who are we now, and why does this heart feel so paralyzed?

Are you the one, the idol that lost its name?
But all they've ever tried to call it, is just another sad phase.
So what are the motives that drive you further than here?
What are the reasons, for all her sad tears?

It pushes us further, all the little words we used to say.
It takes us a little further, when we realize we have no face.
So it brings us down now, into a place we can't recognize.
So is it even logical, all the psycho memories we won't let die?

The Very Worst of Me

What is it in my eyes, that makes you think that I'm mad?
Why is it that every time I smile, you just throw me back?
So what was the point in laughing, if it was all just a lie?
You always thought the worst of me, no matter how hard I tried.

What is it in my words, that makes you think that I'm sad?
Why is it that you always think of me as only a lost man?
So what would the point be, in thinking that it was real?
You always thought the worst of me, now this heart can never heal.

What is it in my thoughts, that just won't let you fade?
Why is it that when you smile, my heart still begins to break?
So what was the point then, in all our hopes and dreams?
No matter what I said, you always thought the very worst of me.

Never She Knew

All the thoughts left lingering, far beyond fear.
As now the tide goes out, and we kiss goodbye another year.
It so tickles inside, the blade that pushes against my heart.
But she never really cared much for me, right from the very start.

It was darker then, when I was waist deep in someone else's blood.
Now I'll never be clean, as I bathe myself in all this mud.
Then it begins to burn a bit, the red line beneath my wrist.
So I just wish I could quit, but I can't escape this fate she wished.

All the thoughts left lingering, far beyond the emotion of doubt.
As now our past is forgotten, lost forever beyond the scattered clouds.
So again it feels like it tickles, the blade that's stuck in my spine.
But never she knew, that in this hell she chose, *"I'll be just fine."*

So What's The Point?

So what's the point now, and why are we all still marching on?
What was the point then, as I waited for you at the dawn?
This life can't make it now, it's too late to say you cared.
So what's the point in trying, when we know you were never there?

So what's the matter now, I can see the sad tears in your eyes?
What did I say my love, please tell me that we'll both be fine?
This life is worthless, so why am I even here if it hurts?
So what was the point then, and tell me when will I ever learn?

So what's the problem today, and why can't I see the light?
So I guess I'm truly to blame, for all these pains we feel at night.
This life is failing, and I don't think I'll make it out today.
So what was the point in living, if it was only for us to fade?

234

I Dive Below

I dive below, in the sea of blood and broken glass.
I sink below, then smile as I take in a very deep breath.
I laugh out loud, but no one cares what I have to say.
So I dive below, hoping the pain will take me away.

I dive below, in the thought of how hard I tried to keep you.
Now I sink to the bottom, knowing I truly have lost my youth.
So I laugh out loud, and smile again in spite of my fate.
So where am I going, I just hope I'm not too late.

I dive below, over my head in the worry of what I am.
I sink below, now stone created from time's eternal sands.
I laugh again, only hoping that someone else is out there.
So I dive below and laugh, as I let out this last breath of air.

Someone Fell Inside

A loud crash, then the lights flickered when she started to scream.
Only one mile left, then I realize I'm only back at the beginning.
A lonely moan, we hear it coming from beneath the stone.
So what are we to do, just let it go and leave it confused?

A thought given once, when we hoped that someday we'd be together.
Now these *tears* are frozen, as I wait alone in this graveyard.
A darker side, in this story of a war in which no one can win.
So what's all of this for, and why won't this mind let it end?

A loud crash, then the lights went out when she started to laugh.
We're only a mile away, then we'll never have to look back.
It's darker now, no colors here where the two of us lie.
But it truly is a sad story, the one of when someone fell inside.

Holding the Moon

She is the only, the light that guides my aching soul.
She holds me soothing, when I realize that I'm all alone.
She is the beacon, that helps me find my way in the dark.
She is my only love, the one that dances with the stars.

She is the only, my love that holds me when I need her touch.
She is all that I desire, in this heart that's filled with only dust.
She is the only path, my past, future and present day.
She holds me soothing, and takes me so very far away.

She is the only, the one who I've been waiting on all my life.
She keeps me blissful, as she guides me deeper into the night.
She is the right choice, and in our eternal love we will be soon.
She is my only faith, so I laugh so joyful while I'm holding the moon.

Eight Rings

It makes me feel like I have a better purpose in this world.
The silver wrapped around eight fingers of this hollow man.
It makes me feel like I have a better role in this story.
But I guess in the end, you won't understand.

It makes me feel like I am the man that I need to be.
The eight silver rings wrapped around the fingers of this hopeless man.
It makes me feel like I am the demon that I've always needed to be.
It makes me whole again so it would be best not to cross me.

It makes me feel like I have a better reason to breathe.
But in the end, you know that you could never understand me.
It makes me feel like I am the one who can make a difference tonight.
It makes me feel like I'm whole again, these eight rings bring me to life.

The Purple

I fall back in my pit of despair, knowing that I have no hope.
I fade back in the smoke, then laugh as I begin to choke.
I feel it winding down, clouding my mind with aches and fear.
So I can only smile now, as I drink down the purple tears.

Behind the torment, I feel the Devil weep as I break.
I find the reason, when I reach inside then lay my heart on a plate.
Behind the whore-bent, we know that justice was only a sham.
Beyond that moment, when you locked me out of all your dreams.

So I fall back once more in this endless void called despair.
I fade back in the smoke, because I know no one's there.
I feel it tearing down, clouding all in this mind with rage and fear.
So again I have to laugh, as I drown in the purple tears.

Questioning Myself

Why is it that no matter what, I still feel it burn?
Why won't the torment stop, and God let me learn?
What was the meaning, to that one muffled thing you said?
When will I just wake up and realize, that I'm already dead?

Who is the one, that's going to be there to laugh when I fall?
What was the sum, and did we even gain anything at all?
So why are we falling, yet still standing in our own heads?
When will God release me, and let me free my last breath?

Why is no one here today, am I wrong to think that I'm alone?
Why won't you forget me, and let me rest forever in this broken hole.
So what was the big reason, why God doesn't care anymore?
When will I wake up and see, what's hiding behind that open door?

Sulfur Tears

Platinum eyes gazing into the hole in my chest.
A hand made of light reaches in but nothing is left.
The angels giggle and smirk at the thought of our lust.
Like clouds it falls in, leaving behind a golden dust.

The burning shards of silver sink now deeper into my wrist.
As I begin to fade away, I kiss God on the lips.
For what is it in my nature, to be so blissful while in pain?
And like drops of fire it falls in, the Devil bleeding an acid rain.

Platinum eyes gazing into the dark cavity in my brain.
A hand made of light reaches out but there's nothing left of me to take.
So all the little angels giggle and grin at the sight of our lusting fears.
So like clouds of acid it falls, bleeding out my sulfur tears.

Fill the Pipe

One two, so here we go - laughing as we fall down the rabbit hole...
It feels insane, as we watch our faces be lost and erased.
It feels so strange, as I wait out here - alone in space.
So what more can I do, what more could I say?

You call it immoral, as I journey deeper into my own world.
Through the smoke then we scamper, hoping to be lost forever more.
You label me as a heretic, so I rip off my shamed face for you.
Now here alone in darkness, I realize that she was untrue.

One two, so here we go - plummeting down the rabbit hole...
Into the insane, that is where your God can find me today.
It feels good, so very good to know I was just a mistake.
So fill the pipe to the top, strike a match and just fade away.

Sadistic

Push me again and watch as I laugh with blood in my throat.
Look close if you can and try to find the hidden note.
The song plays on, so I just sit back and try to relax.
But the nightmare is still looming, and I can never look back.

Push me again and watch as the blood hits the ground.
You try to look at me, as if I were only a heartless clown.
The memory lingers, the thought of when we were divine.
But now we're left with only anger, and it won't ease this mind.

Push me again and try to blink before all the lights fade.
You call me a Devil, a sadistic demon of hate.
The song plays on, so deaf we dance alone.
This nightmare will never end, so please take me home.

Destruction of a Love

I never wanted it to end this way, but it did and that's all I can say.
I've never wished to hurt you my love, so I'm sorry you're in pain.
Was God there watching, as we took that first step over into love?
Does anybody care, for this story of a ghost coming undone?

I never meant to make you feel that way, but in the end I guess you did.
I never wished to make you unhappy, but still we followed on with sin.
Was the Devil laughing, as we said that we would be together forever?
Why does this mind still hurt, please someone find me a better shelter.

I never wanted you to feel the way you did, but now that's passed.
I never thought it'd go this far, so this bullet pushed against my head.
Why am I already burning, and was God there to cast me out?
In hell I lie forever, for the destruction of a love that I denounced.

Are You Happy Now?

The fact is, that there is nowhere left for you to hide.
Try but you'll fail, then weep as you go blind.
Because no matter what they say, you know that it hurts.
So go ahead and try to laugh, as all your memories burn.

The only real grim fact, is that we are truly alone.
And now your head starts to hurt, as you beat it against the stone.
But what was it for, the years of fighting for help.
Now the lights are turned off and you begin to see hell.

The sad but genuine fact is, that you are lost and can't be found.
Go ahead and try it, but I will never truly drown.
There is no one out there, to save you from your fate.
So are you happy now, are you glad we corrected our mistake?

Violent Vendetta

Vulgar velocities vaunting violent vendettas.
Brutal notions resonating as you place a shard into my heart.
All actions of when I loved only you, now gone done and dead.
It was only for a moment but I know I died when you turned your head.

Vicious venom violating various vaulting vendettas.
Cruel as all your words are forgotten when the story fades.
It is because of these actions, that my soul must bear the blame.
Someday you'll understand, why it is I feel this way.

Venting various violent vendettas.
Now the real struggle begins when retribution can't be found.
So on I go in this nightmare, smiling as I fall further down.
It gets me fired up, to think you would do such a thing.
It is truly a hopeless vendetta, and now I know you won't be saved.

A Sheet of Paper

Dancing alone - nine injections away from seeing the light.
Now I know it's freezing, as I suffer my eyes turning to ice.
What choice have I, but to just laugh without any remorse.
I can only sit back now and let damnation take its course.

It's a strange sense, the motions of a demon inside your heart.
It sounds so extraordinary, and then the years begin tearing you apart.
Now truly "*there stands to be more*," and it is time for us to understand the tome.
Just nine injections left, as I dance here all alone.

What did God intend for us and are we fulfilling his egocentric dream?
All thoughts are now left in splinters, but still I hear the scream.
As falling now for a lifetime, realizing "*I'll never get the chance to hit.*"
I know now I'm just a sheet of paper, burning alone as our God had wished.

The Mask Behind the Face

Don't sermonize me with all your false views of faith.
Don't put words in God's mouth, just let him say what he needs to say.
I don't have the time now, to deal with more pointless mistakes.
So I remain forever hidden, hoping all my troubles will just fade.

Don't lecture me with all your opinions of what you call respect.
Load yourself and fade away, because that is what you do best.
I don't have the time now, to be putting up with these senseless pains.
So I hope it to remain lost, the scar covering the vein.

Don't push all your bleak resentments on me today.
Don't try to stand there, and say it was all my mistake.
I don't have the time right now, so please just go away.
So now and forever I remain hidden, the mask behind the face.

Power of the Beast

I feel it glaring, all the loving words of our failed try.
Now it's frozen, stuck forever behind the pointless rhyme.
It's lost and gone now, the hope of being free.
I feel there's no escape now, we are condemned indeed.

I know you're out there, waiting to get your chance.
I saw an angel once, but it was only a small glance.
I feel it pounding now, beating at the back of my eyes.
I know I heard the voice, echoing from deep inside.

The moment passed, now all we have left is our failed try.
Now that I've seen the outcome, I know you were a lie.
It's lost and gone now, the yearning of being set free.
Now I know I feel it rising, the power of the beast.

Acid Reverberations

Over the tip of my eyeball, the blade dances and sings.
Under my fingernails, I can still taste the rotten meat.
What are you looking for, is it the demon that dwells within me?
Beneath my tattered skin, lies a memory that we've never seen.

Over the tip of my tongue, the pills skip and play as they fall down.
Under my broken heart, another rusted needle was found.
What are they truly, the voices that tell me to step over the line?
Now this world is blurry, soon you'll see that the stranger was right.

Over the tip of my spine, the nail is placed and hammered in.
Under my last page, *"I found a half burnt photo of you."*
So what are they truly, all the faces that say they are mine?
Into another shallow pit we fall, only giving it some time.

Over the top and now below the sunken part that was once called me.
In the palm of my hand, remains a love note you wrote so passionately.
What is it really, the missing piece that you think that defines me.
On now it just echoes and echoes, all the reverberations of the acid within me.

Her Hand in His

She was only happy when she was acquiring a bitter lust.
Now everything we've ever strived for, it all turns to dust.
There is nothing left now, so we can only weep in spite.
So I can only laugh, as she smiles and turns off the lights.

She was only happy when her lover gave her everything she required.
Now she's alone with her hand in his and she feels the desire.
There is nothing now that can save this story and give a happy ending.
So I can only now laugh, as I wait here for the beginning.

She was only there for me, because I gave her a chance for hope.
Now in hindsight it seems pointless, as her face fades with the smoke.
There is nothing now, which you can offer to please this mind.
So I can only laugh, and watch my body slowly unwind.

She was only happy when she was getting hers at night.
Now all we do is forget, that perfect moment in our lives.
Because there is nothing now, that can save us from ourselves.
So now I can only laugh at her hand in his, as they both burn in hell...

Double Bladed

Kill it now. Let the tragic memory roll over into my eyes.
Kill your love. Watch as the wax spills over and covers the line.
Kill your spirit. Because life doesn't have time for any of your dreams.
Kill your sanity. And then laugh as God begins to weep.

Hit it harder. Let the blood pour and fill this glass half full.
Hit the gutter. Then wave goodbye as you sink below the pool.
Hit it further. Into darkness is where the ghost led the way.
Hit it once more. Then throw your worn down soul away.

On the other side. That is where I've seen the story end.
On the other line. Led far into the memory of a time within.
On the other chance. Of now you know we can't find the way.
On the other edge you will find me, on this double blade.

Internal Turmoil

Clamoring voices that just want us to say it was right.
A demon howling at the moon, but now he is blind.
Felt once in the middle and now this body seems cold.
What's happening to me within, where did God take my soul?

Racket building louder but my heart won't turn away.
So now I load the gun, just hoping I might be saved.
But the owl is calling, and I know it's my time.
The curtains are falling, and the Devil says it will be fine.

Constant chaos breaking deep into my last nerve.
Numb now and I see, that our dream was so absurd.
I was only trying to prove that I was not only a demon.
But now this internal turmoil sets in, bringing on pure madness.

Doppelganger

Who are you, the face that stares at me from the mirror?
What have I done God, to be tormented for so many years?
I've tried my hardest, but I can't seem to beat the thoughts away.
I want to know you better my friend, my friend wearing my face.

Who are you, the voices that whisper evil notions inside?
What can we say now, what have we left this time?
I've loved you once because you asked me please...
I want now only to die, and set these troubles free.

Who are you, the thoughts that keep this body alive?
What can we say now, I think we're out of time.
I've done my very best, but I wasn't good enough for you.
My lovely friend that waits in the mirror, reminding me it's true...

244

Vomit Dish

My mind can't bare the strain, I think it's coming up.
My heart can't stand the break, so now we're out of luck.
I wish only to see you smile, but you laugh in my face.
You were my only world once, so now I'm stuck in space.

My mind can't hold it any longer, so I think I've reached the end.
I want someone to care for me and shelter this body from sin.
You are right to hate me, because I'm just worthless trash.
I feel it coming up, spreading out over the dish.

Psycho funeral tears are falling, but I know no one cares.
Into the abyss I keep falling, just wishing I was anywhere.
My head is pounding, yet I think I can hold it just a little more.
But now it's spilt over the dish, and spreads onto the floor.

Serrated

I don't have the time, my legs just gave out.
My eyes are getting heavy, so please let me out.
I gave all I can, so I'm sorry I was never enough.
It was a sad ending "yes," now all our memories snuffed.

It pulls across and I know you want me to be there for you.
I think I'm frozen still, laid beneath my tomb.
I feel it tearing, now the bone in clear sight.
In two pieces lies my heart, so you cover it with lime.

I don't want to make you unhappy, but we are dead now today.
My eyes are getting heavy, so maybe I should go to sleep.
Because I've done all I can but still I feel it breaking the skin.
Your serrated blade, cutting so ever gently into this wrist.

Identity Gone

Because I'm the Devil, that is why.
Because I am Satan, your children cry.
I'm the super-demon, forever ruling this hell.
I am the one who was there, and laughed when you fell.

Because I was the Devil, you spat in my face.
Because I was the only one, who had a little faith.
The world can't stand it, the thought of us finding grace.
Now I can only smile, knowing they've stolen my face.

Because I'm the Devil, that is why.
Because you know I am Satan, your children begin to die.
I'm the overlord, forever ruling this depressing hell.
I am the only one that was there, to laugh when they fell.

Cutthroat Smile

Into the darkness this heart begins to slide.
Wake up my love, it's time to open your tired eyes.
It was a great story, but now it's all just passed.
I love the fact that no one cares, and I'm the only one left.

Into the middle part, that's where this mind wanders from *time to time*.
I wish there was more I could say, but I've lost all the rights.
But mother just stands there, waving her hand side to side.
So further now I plummet, into my own spine.

It rips us open, the razor lips pressing against this heart.
Wake up my love, it's time now for you to tear me apart.
It was a great ride, but it's time we just let it go.
So now I just smile back, laughing with this cut throat.

Blade Into Meat

Paste me to the wall, and throw knives at my skull.
Push your fingernails into the flesh and pull it apart.
Lust me now, and lick away all my remaining scars.
It seems so strange, as I eat the soul of another fallen star.

What conceals me better than all the blood and tears?
Why is it only when I'm alone, I can accept my own fears?
Please push your hatred on me and tell me I was just a freak.
Laugh my love with spite, as you place the blade into the meat.

The flames soothe me now, for I have only this option of demise.
You are my only reader, so please wipe clean your tired eyes.
I'm falling further into the madness of days yet to come.
So the blade pushes deeper into the meat, "*God what have I done?*".

Dead Fingers

Fingernails scraping across my spine, pulling the skin back.
You reach beneath the flesh and it feels sharp but then an itch.
I can't seem to grasp it, the fact that we've come this far.
Then the acid drips off the moon and into my aching scars.

Her smile was so great, when she was having a good day.
But the clouds never subsided, so then just constant tears and rain.
It was cold that night, the time when she said goodbye.
Now beneath the mirror, I leave my memories to hide.

Fingernails scraping hard against the bone, so then I laugh.
You reached into my heart, but there was nothing really left.
I've called out to the demon, but I've never got it to react.
Now I have only her dead fingers, digging into my back.

Marijuana Lullabies

Gentle she whispers her lovely voice into my heart.
She warms me with passion, tearing me apart.
I can't reach the ground now, I'm lost somewhere in space.
But no matter where I fall, her touch I would never replace.

Soft as she soothes me, running her fingers through my hair.
Then I feel her kiss, taking away all the air.
I've stepped out of myself, and this is such a neat game.
So I can't help but to laugh, as I rip off my own face.

Gentle she holds me, letting me know she's at my side.
She gropes my heart so soothing, staring into my eyes.
I feel like the floor is melting, eating me alive.
So she kisses me while hoping, that tonight I will survive.

It makes me know she's out there, waiting for me to return.
When I can't feel her soft touch, my heart begins to burn.
She's so great to me, I know she loves me dear.
So as she takes my breath away, God sheds another tear.

Contradiction

Be ready for whatever fate throws your way.
Feel great in the knowing that it's best when you stay.
Say hello to your mother, wear a smile on your face.
Then laugh as she cries and you walk away.

Try as hard as you can, and be there for your neighbors with pride.
Wave at the passing children, and tell them to follow the light.
Take a moment to simply watch, as your life passes you by.
Fight for your freedom, but just be ready to end the ride.

Justice spoke swiftly, then our bodies became ash.
Please tell me why, did we have the audacity to look back.
Now that we're here, let's stand up and speak our minds.
Let's tell the world that we should all live, but only so that we can die...

Stupid Function

Only because you say, that it feels right.
Only when you smile, then turn off the lights.
Only because I love it when you say that I'm the one.
So only a fool would think, that I could be that dumb.

Only if you ask nice, I might show you the last page.
If only someone where here, to remember my face.
Only now it seems that we were walking the right path.
But all your stupid functions, sadly caused us to fall back.

Lust is True

I loved the times, when it was only me and you.
No matter what the world said, we know lust is true.
They try to deny it, but the fact is that we are just beasts.
Reject it all you want but lust has set us free...

I Mean It...

I mean it, there is no way to reach the end of the hall.
I've tried all I can, so now I begin to fall.
Into the endless pit, I watch my heart plummet to hell.
I mean it when I say, this mind is so overwhelmed.

I mean it, you can't stop me now from this point on.
You have no other choice, so just sing along.
Say what you wish, but sanity won't save you this time.
I meant it when I said, you've now crossed the line.

I mean it, just close your mouth then get up and go.
Help me if you wish, to find her beneath the snow.
I know you're unhappy now, but what can I say?
I really mean it, just stay the hell away...

Smoking the Ashes

Kissing the Devil on the lips, then my eyes begin to twitch.
What in God's good name is this inside my head?
I've stepped over now, into the purple world of the lost.
I've been burnt to the bone, now frozen and covered in frost.

I drag my tongue across the coals, winking at the angel.
I take her hand and lead her far beyond all the demon's fables.
What is it in my nature, to enjoy eating the divine alive?
I lie here awake all day, questioning why.

The flesh on the back of my hand begins to boil.
It smells sour yet it tastes just so sweet.
I smile while I kiss the Devil on the lips.
I exhale with a laugh, smoking the ashes to set myself free...

Never Re-Birth

Sky breaking and now it falls against my skull.
The four horsemen ride on, conquering my fragile soul.
I want only to jump, and let my life flash before my eyes.
I want to swim to the bottom and let out a heavy sigh.

The blackness of the yesterday, bitter shadows trying to remain.
It was so many years ago, but somehow I misplaced the grave.
The plague called humanity, we're taking over and that's that.
I want only to smile, I just want to laugh.

Skyward running, hoping that I might reach the moon.
The end is coming, so be ready at noon.
The apocalypse was so great, a painting I'll never forget.
I wish never to be re-born.
I've had more than enough of this...

Edge Of This Mind

A long walk, miles until we reach the last act.
Like a spider-web so thin, we dance on the line into the abyss.
Is that where you want me to go and turn off the lights.
It's been so many years, I hope I can still do it right.

Into the darkness is where this new path leads.
This story is far from over, just open your eyes and see.
We've come far in this journey, and we're not backing down.
I've come to terms now with the fact, I am just a heartless clown.

A long drive if you ask me, we had better leave now.
But what's the point in fighting, when we are already down.
I don't think it'll matter, when the credits begin to roll.
So I stand at the edge of this mind, watching the story unfold...

Last Drag

It's burning, I'm burning, but I cannot just end this.
The nowhere of somewhere, where we all just, we follow.
For nothing and something, we take one more hostage.
I've been there, the ending, where it all just fades away.

Some fear – never clear, when the last drag takes you away.
No tears – while you're here, please hold me once before you go.
Now it's there – please someone care, *I think my heart has gone away.*

You're burning and yearning, for a demon to save you.
You're waiting and hating, because you feel just, so hollow.
I've been there, I've seen it, the mask of the monster.
You hated me, persuaded me, but now I believe in something more.

No cheer – never clear, because this wine we drink is really blood.
No fear – when you're here, so just tell me I'll be okay.
Now it's here – so someone care, as we take our last drag today...

The Circle is Complete

An eagle flies high into the cloudless light-blue sky.
As the sun slowly climbs over the summit of a vast mountain.
With all its elaborate colors shining, as the full moon subsides to sleep.
The animals in nature run free with no fear of each other or me.

A stream turns to a river with the freshly melted snow of a *winter-dawn*.
I was sitting at the river bank on the morning dew-covered grass.
I looked up to watch the eagle soaring free with pride.
The sun breaks the rim of the mountains, and then the world fills with light.

I begin to remember what a wise man once said.
As I've seen what hides behind the open door, leading into destiny.
I stand tall with only nature and the heavens above to hear my cries.
So with a smile I say aloud "it's a good day to die."

The eagle flies, the grass it grows, and the waters flow.

The circle is complete...

Extras:

Spanning through the years 2007 and 2008 this third installment in the series, vocalist/poet Jonathan W. Haubert takes his readers into a new chapter in the twistedly poetic world of the Wars of the Mind. After overcoming his more than a decade long battle with Alcohol & Drug addictions Jonathan W. Haubert headed into studio to begin writing and recording dozens of early demos and rough takes of the "Heavy Metal" vocalist's career in music.

While spending over two years in studio recording, Jonathan W. Haubert's writings had taken on a more lyrical direction and in turn his poetry had become more focused giving Jonathan the ability to use his lyrics and poetry to help find the inner strength to overcome many of his longtime battles. This new chapter in the series Vol.3 (Behind Open Doors.) tells the grim story behind the poet's struggle in finding hope and control. Volume 3 ties together the series while also leading the story into the next chapter of the ongoing poetic adventures, in the Wars of the Mind Vol. 4: (*On-top a Hill – Beneath a Tall Tree.*)

Thanks:

I would like to thank my family and friends.
And again I would like to thank "COUNT YOUR DEAD"
For all these years of great live shows and for all of the years of friendships,
Adventures and !!HEAVY METAL!!

I would like to thank you the reader for joining me once more.
For taking this third journey into the wars of the mind.
And to everyone who picks up this book.
And holds it true to their heart.
"I thank you all."

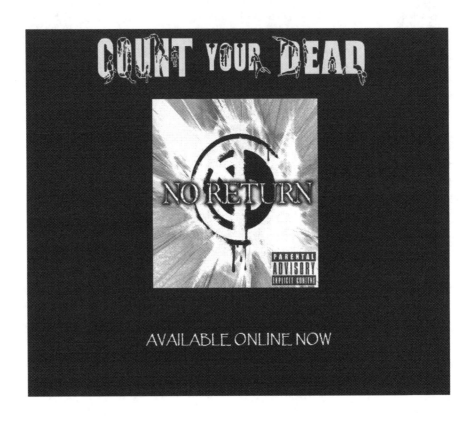

Here I go... Truly having nothing to say.
It took some time... Now we begin to decay.
There I go... Forgotten now and I release.

Coming Soon:

Wars of the Mind
Vol. 4: (*On-top a Hill – Beneath a Tall Tree.*)